TEACHER'S PET PUBLICATIONS

PUZZLE PACK
for
Cheaper by the Dozen
based on the book by
Frank Gilbreth, Jr. & Ernestine Gilbreth Carey

Written by
William T. Collins

© 2005 Teacher's Pet Publications
All Rights Reserved

The materials in this packet are copyrighted
by Teacher's Pet Publications, Inc.

These pages may be duplicated by the purchaser
for use in the purchaser's own classroom.

Copying any of these materials and distributing them
for any other purpose is a violation of the copyright laws.

© 2005 Teacher's Pet Publications, Inc.
www.tpet.com

INTRODUCTION
If you already own the LitPlan for this title, this Puzzle Pack will refresh your Unit Resource Materials and Vocabulary Resource Materials sections plus give you additional materials you can substitute into the tests. If you do not already have a complete LitPlan, these pages will give you some supplemental materials to use with your own plan. There are two main groups of materials: one set for unit words (such as characters' names, symbols, places, etc.) and one set for vocabulary words associated with the book.

WORD LIST
There is a word list for both the unit words and the vocabulary words. These lists show you which words are being used in the materials and the clues or definitions being used for those words. You may want to give students a word list with clues/definitions to help them, or you may want students to only have a word list (without clues/definitions) if you want them to work a little harder. Both are available for duplication. The word lists can also be your "calling key" for the bingo games.

FILL IN THE BLANK AND MATCHING
There are 4 each of the fill in the blank and matching worksheets for both the unit and vocabulary words. These pages can be used either as extra worksheets for students or as objective parts of a unit test. They can be done individually if students need extra help or as a whole class activity to review the material covered.

MAGIC SQUARES
The magic squares not only reinforce the material covered but also work on reasoning and math skills. Many teachers have told us that their students really enjoy doing these!

WORD SEARCH PUZZLES
The word search words go in all directions, as indicated on your answer keys. Two of the word search puzzles have the clues listed rather than the words. This makes the puzzle a little more difficult, but it reinforces the material better. Two word search puzzles have words only for students who find the clue puzzles too difficult.

CROSSWORD PUZZLES
Both unit and vocabulary word sections have 4 crossword puzzles.

BINGO CARDS
There are 32 individual bingo cards for the unit words and 32 individual bingo cards for the vocabulary words. You can use your word list as a "call list," calling the words at random and marking them off of your list as you go, or you could use the flash cards by cutting them apart and drawing the words at random from a hat (or box or whatever). To make a better review, you might ask for the definition and spelling of each word as you call it out–or you could call out the definitions and have students tell you the words they need to look for on the puzzle.

JUGGLE LETTERS
The vocabulary juggle letter game is intended to help students learn the spellings of the words. One sheet has the definitions listed on it as an extra help for students who need it or to reinforce the definitions if you choose to do so.

FLASH CARDS
We've included a set of vocabulary flash cards you can duplicate, cut, and fold for your students. Some teachers make a few sets for general use by the class; others make a set for each student. Some teachers duplicate them for each student and have the students cut & fold their own. You can cut out just the words and put them in a hat, have each student pick out one word and write the definition and a sentence for that word. Students then swap words and papers, with the next student adding a sentence of his own under the last one. You can have students swap as many times as you like. Each time the student will read the sentences written prior to his own and then add a sentence. You can cut out the words and definitions separately and play "I Have; Who Has?" Each student in the room draws a word and definition. The first student says, "I have (the name of the word). Who has the definition?" The student with the definition reads it then says, "I have (the name of the vocabulary word she has). Who has the definition?" The round continues until all words and definitions have been given.

Cheaper By The Dozen Word List

No.	Word	Clue/Definition
1.	ANNE	She bobbed her hair
2.	BATH	The bird ____ was Dad's only failure
3.	BILL	He made Aunt Anne furious by pretending to be a dog
4.	BRICKLAYER	Father began work as a _____'s helper
5.	BURTON	Doctor who got Ernestine and Martha mixed up
6.	CALIFORNIA	State where Mollers lived
7.	CANARIES	Peter and Maggie
8.	CHEAPER	____ By The Dozen
9.	COFFIN	The children buried one full of pencils
10.	COGGIN	He forgot to take the lens cap off the camera, so there were no movies of the tonsillectomy
11.	COUGH	All the children got the whooping ____ on the way home from CA
12.	COUNCIL	The family ___ was set up as a forum for making decisions & voicing grievances
13.	EFFICIENCY	Dad was an ____ expert
14.	ERNESTINE	Co-author; _____ Gilbreth Carey
15.	FLASH	It terrified the children when Father took pictures
16.	FOOLISH	The car; ____ Carriage
17.	GROSIE	She had power over Mother; Mother obeyed her
18.	HEART	Dad had a bad one
19.	JANE	The last baby
20.	JAZZ	Dad did not like the ___ Age
21.	JINGO	Dad's saying; By ____
22.	JOE	He looked like what might happen if a pygmy married a barber pole
23.	KIN	The children thought the Mollers were the kissingest ___ in the world
24.	LANGUAGE	The children studied recorded ____ lessons
25.	LILL	She underbid the others & painted the fence
26.	MAC	Motorcycle ___ was caught peeping in Ernestine's window
27.	MARTHA	She learned to do math quickly in her head
28.	MEASLES	Father put red ink spots on his face, pretending to have ___
29.	MEBANE	She tried to organize a group of women to be advocates of birth control
30.	MOLLERS	They were Mother's family
31.	MORSE	Father painted messages on the walls in ___ code
32.	MOTION	Dad's occupation; ___ study
33.	POOR	Over the hill and to the ___ house
34.	PSYCHOLOGIST	The children tried to make him think they were horribly maladjusted
35.	RENA	The boat
36.	SHOE	Name for the cottage
37.	SUNDAY	The children went to ___ school because Mr. Gilbreth wanted them to have a well-rounded education
38.	TEA	At the ___ party the kids got tired of being angels & jumped into the sprinkler water
39.	THERBLIG	A unit of motion or thought
40.	TONSILS	The children and Dad had theirs removed
41.	TYPEWRITER	It was named Moby Dick
42.	WHISTLE	Signal for everyone to gather

Cheaper By The Dozen Fill In The Blank 1

_____ 1. He looked like what might happen if a pygmy married a barber pole
_____ 2. The children went to ___ school because Mr. Gilbreth wanted them to have a well-rounded education
_____ 3. It was named Moby Dick
_____ 4. She underbid the others & painted the fence
_____ 5. Dad had a bad one
_____ 6. Dad's saying; By ____
_____ 7. He made Aunt Anne furious by pretending to be a dog
_____ 8. It terrified the children when Father took pictures
_____ 9. Dad was an ____ expert
_____ 10. ____ By The Dozen
_____ 11. Co-author; _____ Gilbreth Carey
_____ 12. He forgot to take the lens cap off the camera, so there were no movies of the tonsillectomy
_____ 13. Father painted messages on the walls in ___ code
_____ 14. At the ___ party the kids got tired of being angels & jumped into the sprinkler water
_____ 15. The car; ____ Carriage
_____ 16. She bobbed her hair
_____ 17. The children and Dad had theirs removed
_____ 18. Doctor who got Ernestine and Martha mixed up
_____ 19. The children thought the Mollers were the kissingest ___ in the world
_____ 20. She learned to do math quickly in her head

Cheaper By The Dozen Fill In The Blank 1 Answer Key

JOE	1. He looked like what might happen if a pygmy married a barber pole
SUNDAY	2. The children went to ___ school because Mr. Gilbreth wanted them to have a well-rounded education
TYPEWRITER	3. It was named Moby Dick
LILL	4. She underbid the others & painted the fence
HEART	5. Dad had a bad one
JINGO	6. Dad's saying; By ____
BILL	7. He made Aunt Anne furious by pretending to be a dog
FLASH	8. It terrified the children when Father took pictures
EFFICIENCY	9. Dad was an ____ expert
CHEAPER	10. ____ By The Dozen
ERNESTINE	11. Co-author; _____ Gilbreth Carey
COGGIN	12. He forgot to take the lens cap off the camera, so there were no movies of the tonsillectomy
MORSE	13. Father painted messages on the walls in ___ code
TEA	14. At the ___ party the kids got tired of being angels & jumped into the sprinkler water
FOOLISH	15. The car; ____ Carriage
ANNE	16. She bobbed her hair
TONSILS	17. The children and Dad had theirs removed
BURTON	18. Doctor who got Ernestine and Martha mixed up
KIN	19. The children thought the Mollers were the kissingest ___ in the world
MARTHA	20. She learned to do math quickly in her head

Cheaper By The Dozen Fill In The Blank 2

1. The car; ____ Carriage
2. She tried to organize a group of women to be advocates of birth control
3. ____ By The Dozen
4. Signal for everyone to gather
5. The boat
6. Peter and Maggie
7. The last baby
8. He forgot to take the lens cap off the camera, so there were no movies of the tonsillectomy
9. State where Mollers lived
10. Father began work as a _____'s helper
11. The children buried one full of pencils
12. A unit of motion or thought
13. It was named Moby Dick
14. Over the hill and to the ___ house
15. Dad had a bad one
16. The children went to ___ school because Mr. Gilbreth wanted them to have a well-rounded education
17. Name for the cottage
18. Dad's saying; By ____
19. She had power over Mother; Mother obeyed her
20. Doctor who got Ernestine and Martha mixed up

Cheaper By The Dozen Fill In The Blank 2 Answer Key

FOOLISH	1. The car; ____ Carriage
MEBANE	2. She tried to organize a group of women to be advocates of birth control
CHEAPER	3. ____ By The Dozen
WHISTLE	4. Signal for everyone to gather
RENA	5. The boat
CANARIES	6. Peter and Maggie
JANE	7. The last baby
COGGIN	8. He forgot to take the lens cap off the camera, so there were no movies of the tonsillectomy
CALIFORNIA	9. State where Mollers lived
BRICKLAYER	10. Father began work as a _____'s helper
COFFIN	11. The children buried one full of pencils
THERBLIG	12. A unit of motion or thought
TYPEWRITER	13. It was named Moby Dick
POOR	14. Over the hill and to the ___ house
HEART	15. Dad had a bad one
SUNDAY	16. The children went to ___ school because Mr. Gilbreth wanted them to have a well-rounded education
SHOE	17. Name for the cottage
JINGO	18. Dad's saying; By ____
GROSIE	19. She had power over Mother; Mother obeyed her
BURTON	20. Doctor who got Ernestine and Martha mixed up

Cheaper By The Dozen Fill In The Blank 3

1. The children and Dad had theirs removed
2. Over the hill and to the ___ house
3. The children buried one full of pencils
4. A unit of motion or thought
5. Co-author; _____ Gilbreth Carey
6. Dad's occupation; ___ study
7. ____ By The Dozen
8. It was named Moby Dick
9. State where Mollers lived
10. The children tried to make him think they were horribly maladjusted
11. Father painted messages on the walls in ___ code
12. Peter and Maggie
13. The children went to ___ school because Mr. Gilbreth wanted them to have a well-rounded education
14. She bobbed her hair
15. She tried to organize a group of women to be advocates of birth control
16. Dad was an ____ expert
17. The last baby
18. All the children got the whooping ____ on the way home from CA
19. He looked like what might happen if a pygmy married a barber pole
20. They were Mother's family

Cheaper By The Dozen Fill In The Blank 3 Answer Key

TONSILS	1. The children and Dad had theirs removed
POOR	2. Over the hill and to the ___ house
COFFIN	3. The children buried one full of pencils
THERBLIG	4. A unit of motion or thought
ERNESTINE	5. Co-author; _____ Gilbreth Carey
MOTION	6. Dad's occupation; ___ study
CHEAPER	7. ____ By The Dozen
TYPEWRITER	8. It was named Moby Dick
CALIFORNIA	9. State where Mollers lived
PSYCHOLOGIST	10. The children tried to make him think they were horribly maladjusted
MORSE	11. Father painted messages on the walls in ___ code
CANARIES	12. Peter and Maggie
SUNDAY	13. The children went to ___ school because Mr. Gilbreth wanted them to have a well-rounded education
ANNE	14. She bobbed her hair
MEBANE	15. She tried to organize a group of women to be advocates of birth control
EFFICIENCY	16. Dad was an ____ expert
JANE	17. The last baby
COUGH	18. All the children got the whooping ____ on the way home from CA
JOE	19. He looked like what might happen if a pygmy married a barber pole
MOLLERS	20. They were Mother's family

Cheaper By The Dozen Fill In The Blank 4

1. State where Mollers lived
2. She learned to do math quickly in her head
3. The children and Dad had theirs removed
4. Father painted messages on the walls in ___ code
5. She underbid the others & painted the fence
6. All the children got the whooping ____ on the way home from CA
7. Doctor who got Ernestine and Martha mixed up
8. Motorcycle ___ was caught peeping in Ernestine's window
9. It was named Moby Dick
10. She bobbed her hair
11. Peter and Maggie
12. The children tried to make him think they were horribly maladjusted
13. The car; ____ Carriage
14. The boat
15. The children went to ___ school because Mr. Gilbreth wanted them to have a well-rounded education
16. He forgot to take the lens cap off the camera, so there were no movies of the tonsillectomy
17. Dad was an ____ expert
18. The last baby
19. Father began work as a _____'s helper
20. They were Mother's family

Cheaper By The Dozen Fill In The Blank 4 Answer Key

CALIFORNIA	1. State where Mollers lived
MARTHA	2. She learned to do math quickly in her head
TONSILS	3. The children and Dad had theirs removed
MORSE	4. Father painted messages on the walls in ___ code
LILL	5. She underbid the others & painted the fence
COUGH	6. All the children got the whooping ____ on the way home from CA
BURTON	7. Doctor who got Ernestine and Martha mixed up
MAC	8. Motorcycle ___ was caught peeping in Ernestine's window
TYPEWRITER	9. It was named Moby Dick
ANNE	10. She bobbed her hair
CANARIES	11. Peter and Maggie
PSYCHOLOGIST	12. The children tried to make him think they were horribly maladjusted
FOOLISH	13. The car; ____ Carriage
RENA	14. The boat
SUNDAY	15. The children went to ___ school because Mr. Gilbreth wanted them to have a well-rounded education
COGGIN	16. He forgot to take the lens cap off the camera, so there were no movies of the tonsillectomy
EFFICIENCY	17. Dad was an ____ expert
JANE	18. The last baby
BRICKLAYER	19. Father began work as a _____'s helper
MOLLERS	20. They were Mother's family

Cheaper By The Dozen Matching 1

___ 1. CALIFORNIA   A. Peter and Maggie

___ 2. ERNESTINE   B. Dad did not like the ___ Age

___ 3. MORSE   C. State where Mollers lived

___ 4. JAZZ   D. She learned to do math quickly in her head

___ 5. BURTON   E. Dad's occupation; ___ study

___ 6. MOTION   F. She tried to organize a group of women to be advocates of birth control

___ 7. THERBLIG   G. Dad was an ____ expert

___ 8. ANNE   H. They were Mother's family

___ 9. BRICKLAYER   I. Doctor who got Ernestine and Martha mixed up

___ 10. JINGO   J. The children thought the Mollers were the kissingest ___ in the world

___ 11. MEBANE   K. The family ___ was set up as a forum for making decisions & voicing grievances

___ 12. EFFICIENCY   L. Father painted messages on the walls in ___ code

___ 13. GROSIE   M. Co-author; _____ Gilbreth Carey

___ 14. COUNCIL   N. She had power over Mother; Mother obeyed her

___ 15. SHOE   O. It was named Moby Dick

___ 16. MAC   P. The children tried to make him think they were horribly maladjusted

___ 17. JOE   Q. He forgot to take the lens cap off the camera, so there were no movies of the tonsillectomy

___ 18. KIN   R. He looked like what might happen if a pygmy married a barber pole

___ 19. COFFIN   S. Father began work as a _____'s helper

___ 20. MOLLERS   T. A unit of motion or thought

___ 21. CANARIES   U. She bobbed her hair

___ 22. COGGIN   V. Name for the cottage

___ 23. PSYCHOLOGIST   W. Dad's saying; By ____

___ 24. MARTHA   X. The children buried one full of pencils

___ 25. TYPEWRITER   Y. Motorcycle ___ was caught peeping in Ernestine's window

Cheaper By The Dozen Matching 1 Answer Key

C - 1. CALIFORNIA   A. Peter and Maggie
M - 2. ERNESTINE   B. Dad did not like the ___ Age
L - 3. MORSE   C. State where Mollers lived
B - 4. JAZZ   D. She learned to do math quickly in her head
I - 5. BURTON   E. Dad's occupation; ___ study
E - 6. MOTION   F. She tried to organize a group of women to be advocates of birth control
T - 7. THERBLIG   G. Dad was an ____ expert
U - 8. ANNE   H. They were Mother's family
S - 9. BRICKLAYER   I. Doctor who got Ernestine and Martha mixed up
W -10. JINGO   J. The children thought the Mollers were the kissingest ___ in the world
F -11. MEBANE   K. The family ___ was set up as a forum for making decisions & voicing grievances
G -12. EFFICIENCY   L. Father painted messages on the walls in ___ code
N -13. GROSIE   M. Co-author; _____ Gilbreth Carey
K -14. COUNCIL   N. She had power over Mother; Mother obeyed her
V -15. SHOE   O. It was named Moby Dick
Y -16. MAC   P. The children tried to make him think they were horribly maladjusted
R -17. JOE   Q. He forgot to take the lens cap off the camera, so there were no movies of the tonsillectomy
J -18. KIN   R. He looked like what might happen if a pygmy married a barber pole
X -19. COFFIN   S. Father began work as a _____'s helper
H -20. MOLLERS   T. A unit of motion or thought
A -21. CANARIES   U. She bobbed her hair
Q -22. COGGIN   V. Name for the cottage
P -23. PSYCHOLOGIST   W. Dad's saying; By ____
D -24. MARTHA   X. The children buried one full of pencils
O -25. TYPEWRITER   Y. Motorcycle ___ was caught peeping in Ernestine's window

Cheaper By The Dozen Matching 2

___ 1. BATH
___ 2. JAZZ
___ 3. LANGUAGE
___ 4. POOR
___ 5. SHOE
___ 6. RENA
___ 7. GROSIE
___ 8. MEBANE
___ 9. TYPEWRITER
___ 10. COUGH
___ 11. MOTION
___ 12. COFFIN
___ 13. COUNCIL
___ 14. CALIFORNIA
___ 15. CHEAPER
___ 16. TEA
___ 17. TONSILS
___ 18. MOLLERS
___ 19. WHISTLE
___ 20. JANE
___ 21. ERNESTINE
___ 22. BILL
___ 23. KIN
___ 24. EFFICIENCY
___ 25. HEART

A. Dad had a bad one
B. The last baby
C. Signal for everyone to gather
D. She had power over Mother; Mother obeyed her
E. The children buried one full of pencils
F. Dad's occupation; ___ study
G. All the children got the whooping ___ on the way home from CA
H. She tried to organize a group of women to be advocates of birth control
I. Co-author; _____ Gilbreth Carey
J. Name for the cottage
K. They were Mother's family
L. It was named Moby Dick
M. Dad did not like the ___ Age
N. The children and Dad had theirs removed
O. The bird ___ was Dad's only failure
P. State where Mollers lived
Q. Dad was an ____ expert
R. The children thought the Mollers were the kissingest ___ in the world
S. The family ___ was set up as a forum for making decisions & voicing grievances
T. The boat
U. The children studied recorded ____ lessons
V. Over the hill and to the ___ house
W. ____ By The Dozen
X. At the ___ party the kids got tired of being angels & jumped into the sprinkler water
Y. He made Aunt Anne furious by pretending to be a dog

Cheaper By The Dozen Matching 2 Answer Key

O - 1. BATH	A.	Dad had a bad one
M - 2. JAZZ	B.	The last baby
U - 3. LANGUAGE	C.	Signal for everyone to gather
V - 4. POOR	D.	She had power over Mother; Mother obeyed her
J - 5. SHOE	E.	The children buried one full of pencils
T - 6. RENA	F.	Dad's occupation; ___ study
D - 7. GROSIE	G.	All the children got the whooping ____ on the way home from CA
H - 8. MEBANE	H.	She tried to organize a group of women to be advocates of birth control
L - 9. TYPEWRITER	I.	Co-author; _____ Gilbreth Carey
G -10. COUGH	J.	Name for the cottage
F -11. MOTION	K.	They were Mother's family
E -12. COFFIN	L.	It was named Moby Dick
S -13. COUNCIL	M.	Dad did not like the ___ Age
P -14. CALIFORNIA	N.	The children and Dad had theirs removed
W -15. CHEAPER	O.	The bird ___ was Dad's only failure
X -16. TEA	P.	State where Mollers lived
N -17. TONSILS	Q.	Dad was an ____ expert
K -18. MOLLERS	R.	The children thought the Mollers were the kissingest ___ in the world
C -19. WHISTLE	S.	The family ___ was set up as a forum for making decisions & voicing grievances
B -20. JANE	T.	The boat
I - 21. ERNESTINE	U.	The children studied recorded ____ lessons
Y -22. BILL	V.	Over the hill and to the ___ house
R -23. KIN	W.	____ By The Dozen
Q -24. EFFICIENCY	X.	At the ___ party the kids got tired of being angels & jumped into the sprinkler water
A -25. HEART	Y.	He made Aunt Anne furious by pretending to be a dog

Cheaper By The Dozen Matching 3

___ 1. POOR
___ 2. BURTON
___ 3. TEA
___ 4. CHEAPER
___ 5. EFFICIENCY
___ 6. COGGIN
___ 7. SHOE
___ 8. MOLLERS
___ 9. PSYCHOLOGIST
___ 10. JOE
___ 11. RENA
___ 12. COFFIN
___ 13. THERBLIG
___ 14. LANGUAGE
___ 15. KIN
___ 16. LILL
___ 17. COUNCIL
___ 18. JANE
___ 19. BATH
___ 20. HEART
___ 21. BILL
___ 22. MEBANE
___ 23. MOTION
___ 24. MAC
___ 25. JAZZ

A. Over the hill and to the ___ house
B. He looked like what might happen if a pygmy married a barber pole
C. Motorcycle ___ was caught peeping in Ernestine's window
D. Dad did not like the ___ Age
E. ___ By The Dozen
F. She tried to organize a group of women to be advocates of birth control
G. The family ___ was set up as a forum for making decisions & voicing grievances
H. The children studied recorded ___ lessons
I. Dad was an ___ expert
J. Dad's occupation; ___ study
K. Doctor who got Ernestine and Martha mixed up
L. The last baby
M. She underbid the others & painted the fence
N. The children thought the Mollers were the kissingest ___ in the world
O. At the ___ party the kids got tired of being angels & jumped into the sprinkler water
P. He forgot to take the lens cap off the camera, so there were no movies of the tonsillectomy
Q. Name for the cottage
R. The boat
S. The children tried to make him think they were horribly maladjusted
T. They were Mother's family
U. Dad had a bad one
V. The bird ___ was Dad's only failure
W. He made Aunt Anne furious by pretending to be a dog
X. A unit of motion or thought
Y. The children buried one full of pencils

Cheaper By The Dozen Matching 3 Answer Key

A - 1. POOR	A.	Over the hill and to the ___ house
K - 2. BURTON	B.	He looked like what might happen if a pygmy married a barber pole
O - 3. TEA	C.	Motorcycle ___ was caught peeping in Ernestine's window
E - 4. CHEAPER	D.	Dad did not like the ___ Age
I - 5. EFFICIENCY	E.	___ By The Dozen
P - 6. COGGIN	F.	She tried to organize a group of women to be advocates of birth control
Q - 7. SHOE	G.	The family ___ was set up as a forum for making decisions & voicing grievances
T - 8. MOLLERS	H.	The children studied recorded ___ lessons
S - 9. PSYCHOLOGIST	I.	Dad was an ___ expert
B - 10. JOE	J.	Dad's occupation; ___ study
R - 11. RENA	K.	Doctor who got Ernestine and Martha mixed up
Y - 12. COFFIN	L.	The last baby
X - 13. THERBLIG	M.	She underbid the others & painted the fence
H - 14. LANGUAGE	N.	The children thought the Mollers were the kissingest ___ in the world
N - 15. KIN	O.	At the ___ party the kids got tired of being angels & jumped into the sprinkler water
M - 16. LILL	P.	He forgot to take the lens cap off the camera, so there were no movies of the tonsillectomy
G - 17. COUNCIL	Q.	Name for the cottage
L - 18. JANE	R.	The boat
V - 19. BATH	S.	The children tried to make him think they were horribly maladjusted
U - 20. HEART	T.	They were Mother's family
W - 21. BILL	U.	Dad had a bad one
F - 22. MEBANE	V.	The bird ___ was Dad's only failure
J - 23. MOTION	W.	He made Aunt Anne furious by pretending to be a dog
C - 24. MAC	X.	A unit of motion or thought
D - 25. JAZZ	Y.	The children buried one full of pencils

Cheaper By The Dozen Matching 4

___ 1. WHISTLE
___ 2. MORSE
___ 3. TONSILS
___ 4. JAZZ
___ 5. CALIFORNIA
___ 6. COFFIN
___ 7. TEA
___ 8. RENA
___ 9. MAC
___ 10. MOLLERS
___ 11. TYPEWRITER
___ 12. COGGIN
___ 13. KIN
___ 14. POOR
___ 15. BURTON
___ 16. MOTION
___ 17. FOOLISH
___ 18. THERBLIG
___ 19. BRICKLAYER
___ 20. ANNE
___ 21. SUNDAY
___ 22. CANARIES
___ 23. COUNCIL
___ 24. EFFICIENCY
___ 25. FLASH

A. The children and Dad had theirs removed
B. He forgot to take the lens cap off the camera, so there were no movies of the tonsillectomy
C. The car; ____ Carriage
D. The children buried one full of pencils
E. The children thought the Mollers were the kissingest ___ in the world
F. It terrified the children when Father took pictures
G. Dad's occupation; ___ study
H. Dad was an ____ expert
I. Over the hill and to the ___ house
J. Father painted messages on the walls in ___ code
K. Peter and Maggie
L. It was named Moby Dick
M. They were Mother's family
N. Father began work as a _____'s helper
O. Dad did not like the ___ Age
P. Signal for everyone to gather
Q. Doctor who got Ernestine and Martha mixed up
R. She bobbed her hair
S. The family ___ was set up as a forum for making decisions & voicing grievances
T. Motorcycle ___ was caught peeping in Ernestine's window
U. At the ___ party the kids got tired of being angels & jumped into the sprinkler water
V. The boat
W. A unit of motion or thought
X. State where Mollers lived
Y. The children went to ___ school because Mr. Gilbreth wanted them to have a well-rounded education

Cheaper By The Dozen Matching 4 Answer Key

P - 1.	WHISTLE	A. The children and Dad had theirs removed
J - 2.	MORSE	B. He forgot to take the lens cap off the camera, so there were no movies of the tonsillectomy
A - 3.	TONSILS	C. The car; ____ Carriage
O - 4.	JAZZ	D. The children buried one full of pencils
X - 5.	CALIFORNIA	E. The children thought the Mollers were the kissingest ___ in the world
D - 6.	COFFIN	F. It terrified the children when Father took pictures
U - 7.	TEA	G. Dad's occupation; ___ study
V - 8.	RENA	H. Dad was an ____ expert
T - 9.	MAC	I. Over the hill and to the ___ house
M - 10.	MOLLERS	J. Father painted messages on the walls in ___ code
L - 11.	TYPEWRITER	K. Peter and Maggie
B - 12.	COGGIN	L. It was named Moby Dick
E - 13.	KIN	M. They were Mother's family
I - 14.	POOR	N. Father began work as a _____'s helper
Q - 15.	BURTON	O. Dad did not like the ___ Age
G - 16.	MOTION	P. Signal for everyone to gather
C - 17.	FOOLISH	Q. Doctor who got Ernestine and Martha mixed up
W - 18.	THERBLIG	R. She bobbed her hair
N - 19.	BRICKLAYER	S. The family ___ was set up as a forum for making decisions & voicing grievances
R - 20.	ANNE	T. Motorcycle ___ was caught peeping in Ernestine's window
Y - 21.	SUNDAY	U. At the ___ party the kids got tired of being angels & jumped into the sprinkler water
K - 22.	CANARIES	V. The boat
S - 23.	COUNCIL	W. A unit of motion or thought
H - 24.	EFFICIENCY	X. State where Mollers lived
F - 25.	FLASH	Y. The children went to ___ school because Mr. Gilbreth wanted them to have a well-rounded education

Cheaper By The Dozen Magic Squares 1

Match the definition with the vocabulary word. Put your answers in the magic squares below. When your answers are correct, all columns and rows will add to the same number.

A. SUNDAY
B. GROSIE
C. SHOE
D. JANE
E. CHEAPER
F. POOR
G. COUGH
H. MEBANE
I. COGGIN
J. FLASH
K. MOLLERS
L. ERNESTINE
M. CALIFORNIA
N. MORSE
O. WHISTLE
P. TEA

1. Signal for everyone to gather
2. It terrified the children when Father took pictures
3. She tried to organize a group of women to be advocates of birth control
4. The children went to ___ school because Mr. Gilbreth wanted them to have a well-rounded education
5. The last baby
6. ____ By The Dozen
7. They were Mother's family
8. Father painted messages on the walls in ___ code
9. Over the hill and to the ___ house
10. Name for the cottage
11. State where Mollers lived
12. Co-author; _____ Gilbreth Carey
13. He forgot to take the lens cap off the camera, so there were no movies of the tonsillectomy
14. At the ___ party the kids got tired of being angels & jumped into the sprinkler water
15. She had power over Mother; Mother obeyed her
16. All the children got the whooping ____ on the way home from CA

A=	B=	C=	D=
E=	F=	G=	H=
I=	J=	K=	L=
M=	N=	O=	P=

Cheaper By The Dozen Magic Squares 1 Answer Key

Match the definition with the vocabulary word. Put your answers in the magic squares below. When your answers are correct, all columns and rows will add to the same number.

A. SUNDAY
B. GROSIE
C. SHOE
D. JANE
E. CHEAPER
F. POOR
G. COUGH
H. MEBANE
I. COGGIN
J. FLASH
K. MOLLERS
L. ERNESTINE
M. CALIFORNIA
N. MORSE
O. WHISTLE
P. TEA

1. Signal for everyone to gather
2. It terrified the children when Father took pictures
3. She tried to organize a group of women to be advocates of birth control
4. The children went to ___ school because Mr. Gilbreth wanted them to have a well-rounded education
5. The last baby
6. ____ By The Dozen
7. They were Mother's family
8. Father painted messages on the walls in ___ code
9. Over the hill and to the ___ house
10. Name for the cottage
11. State where Mollers lived
12. Co-author; _____ Gilbreth Carey
13. He forgot to take the lens cap off the camera, so there were no movies of the tonsillectomy
14. At the ___ party the kids got tired of being angels & jumped into the sprinkler water
15. She had power over Mother; Mother obeyed her
16. All the children got the whooping ____ on the way home from CA

A=4	B=15	C=10	D=5
E=6	F=9	G=16	H=3
I=13	J=2	K=7	L=12
M=11	N=8	O=1	P=14

Cheaper By The Dozen Magic Squares 2

Match the definition with the vocabulary word. Put your answers in the magic squares below. When your answers are correct, all columns and rows will add to the same number.

A. KIN
B. TEA
C. MOLLERS
D. CALIFORNIA
E. TYPEWRITER
F. SUNDAY
G. ANNE
H. JOE
I. TONSILS
J. CANARIES
K. MEASLES
L. EFFICIENCY
M. JINGO
N. MAC
O. COGGIN
P. PSYCHOLOGIST

1. He looked like what might happen if a pygmy married a barber pole
2. Dad's saying; By ____
3. At the ___ party the kids got tired of being angels & jumped into the sprinkler water
4. Father put red ink spots on his face, pretending to have ___
5. Peter and Maggie
6. They were Mother's family
7. The children tried to make him think they were horribly maladjusted
8. It was named Moby Dick
9. He forgot to take the lens cap off the camera, so there were no movies of the tonsillectomy
10. The children went to ___ school because Mr. Gilbreth wanted them to have a well-rounded education
11. The children and Dad had theirs removed
12. State where Mollers lived
13. The children thought the Mollers were the kissingest ___ in the world
14. Dad was an ____ expert
15. She bobbed her hair
16. Motorcycle ___ was caught peeping in Ernestine's window

A=	B=	C=	D=
E=	F=	G=	H=
I=	J=	K=	L=
M=	N=	O=	P=

Cheaper By The Dozen Magic Squares 2 Answer Key

Match the definition with the vocabulary word. Put your answers in the magic squares below. When your answers are correct, all columns and rows will add to the same number.

A. KIN
B. TEA
C. MOLLERS
D. CALIFORNIA
E. TYPEWRITER
F. SUNDAY
G. ANNE
H. JOE
I. TONSILS
J. CANARIES
K. MEASLES
L. EFFICIENCY
M. JINGO
N. MAC
O. COGGIN
P. PSYCHOLOGIST

1. He looked like what might happen if a pygmy married a barber pole
2. Dad's saying; By ____
3. At the ___ party the kids got tired of being angels & jumped into the sprinkler water
4. Father put red ink spots on his face, pretending to have ___
5. Peter and Maggie
6. They were Mother's family
7. The children tried to make him think they were horribly maladjusted
8. It was named Moby Dick
9. He forgot to take the lens cap off the camera, so there were no movies of the tonsillectomy
10. The children went to ___ school because Mr. Gilbreth wanted them to have a well-rounded education
11. The children and Dad had theirs removed
12. State where Mollers lived
13. The children thought the Mollers were the kissingest ___ in the world
14. Dad was an ____ expert
15. She bobbed her hair
16. Motorcycle ___ was caught peeping in Ernestine's window

A=13	B=3	C=6	D=12
E=8	F=10	G=15	H=1
I=11	J=5	K=4	L=14
M=2	N=16	O=9	P=7

Cheaper By The Dozen Magic Squares 3

Match the definition with the vocabulary word. Put your answers in the magic squares below. When your answers are correct, all columns and rows will add to the same number.

A. GROSIE
B. COGGIN
C. MEASLES
D. COUGH
E. MOLLERS
F. EFFICIENCY
G. HEART
H. JANE
I. THERBLIG
J. BURTON
K. CHEAPER
L. MARTHA
M. BRICKLAYER
N. MEBANE
O. MOTION
P. LANGUAGE

1. Dad was an _____ expert
2. A unit of motion or thought
3. Dad's occupation; ___ study
4. All the children got the whooping _____ on the way home from CA
5. Father began work as a _____'s helper
6. He forgot to take the lens cap off the camera, so there were no movies of the tonsillectomy
7. The last baby
8. _____ By The Dozen
9. Father put red ink spots on his face, pretending to have ___
10. The children studied recorded _____ lessons
11. Doctor who got Ernestine and Martha mixed up
12. They were Mother's family
13. She learned to do math quickly in her head
14. Dad had a bad one
15. She had power over Mother; Mother obeyed her
16. She tried to organize a group of women to be advocates of birth control

A=	B=	C=	D=
E=	F=	G=	H=
I=	J=	K=	L=
M=	N=	O=	P=

Cheaper By The Dozen Magic Squares 3 Answer Key

Match the definition with the vocabulary word. Put your answers in the magic squares below. When your answers are correct, all columns and rows will add to the same number.

A. GROSIE
B. COGGIN
C. MEASLES
D. COUGH
E. MOLLERS
F. EFFICIENCY
G. HEART
H. JANE
I. THERBLIG
J. BURTON
K. CHEAPER
L. MARTHA
M. BRICKLAYER
N. MEBANE
O. MOTION
P. LANGUAGE

1. Dad was an ____ expert
2. A unit of motion or thought
3. Dad's occupation; ____ study
4. All the children got the whooping ____ on the way home from CA
5. Father began work as a _____'s helper
6. He forgot to take the lens cap off the camera, so there were no movies of the tonsillectomy
7. The last baby
8. ____ By The Dozen
9. Father put red ink spots on his face, pretending to have ___
10. The children studied recorded ____ lessons
11. Doctor who got Ernestine and Martha mixed up
12. They were Mother's family
13. She learned to do math quickly in her head
14. Dad had a bad one
15. She had power over Mother; Mother obeyed her
16. She tried to organize a group of women to be advocates of birth control

A=15	B=6	C=9	D=4
E=12	F=1	G=14	H=7
I=2	J=11	K=8	L=13
M=5	N=16	O=3	P=10

Cheaper By The Dozen Magic Squares 4

Match the definition with the vocabulary word. Put your answers in the magic squares below. When your answers are correct, all columns and rows will add to the same number.

A. JOE
B. TEA
C. CHEAPER
D. FLASH
E. COUGH
F. MAC
G. JINGO
H. MORSE
I. COGGIN
J. FOOLISH
K. LILL
L. PSYCHOLOGIST
M. MOTION
N. COUNCIL
O. MOLLERS
P. BATH

1. He looked like what might happen if a pygmy married a barber pole
2. The family ___ was set up as a forum for making decisions & voicing grievances
3. The car; ____ Carriage
4. All the children got the whooping ____ on the way home from CA
5. Dad's saying; By ____
6. The children tried to make him think they were horribly maladjusted
7. The bird ___ was Dad's only failure
8. ____ By The Dozen
9. They were Mother's family
10. It terrified the children when Father took pictures
11. Father painted messages on the walls in ___ code
12. She underbid the others & painted the fence
13. He forgot to take the lens cap off the camera, so there were no movies of the tonsillectomy
14. Motorcycle ___ was caught peeping in Ernestine's window
15. At the ___ party the kids got tired of being angels & jumped into the sprinkler water
16. Dad's occupation; ___ study

A=	B=	C=	D=
E=	F=	G=	H=
I=	J=	K=	L=
M=	N=	O=	P=

Cheaper By The Dozen Magic Squares 4 Answer Key

Match the definition with the vocabulary word. Put your answers in the magic squares below. When your answers are correct, all columns and rows will add to the same number.

A. JOE
B. TEA
C. CHEAPER
D. FLASH
E. COUGH
F. MAC
G. JINGO
H. MORSE
I. COGGIN
J. FOOLISH
K. LILL
L. PSYCHOLOGIST
M. MOTION
N. COUNCIL
O. MOLLERS
P. BATH

1. He looked like what might happen if a pygmy married a barber pole
2. The family ___ was set up as a forum for making decisions & voicing grievances
3. The car; ____ Carriage
4. All the children got the whooping ____ on the way home from CA
5. Dad's saying; By ____
6. The children tried to make him think they were horribly maladjusted
7. The bird ___ was Dad's only failure
8. ____ By The Dozen
9. They were Mother's family
10. It terrified the children when Father took pictures
11. Father painted messages on the walls in ___ code
12. She underbid the others & painted the fence
13. He forgot to take the lens cap off the camera, so there were no movies of the tonsillectomy
14. Motorcycle ___ was caught peeping in Ernestine's window
15. At the ___ party the kids got tired of being angels & jumped into the sprinkler water
16. Dad's occupation; ___ study

A=1	B=15	C=8	D=10
E=4	F=14	G=5	H=11
I=13	J=3	K=12	L=6
M=16	N=2	O=9	P=7

Cheaper By The Dozen Word Search 1

```
H L W M Y H J T M Y W F L A S H L W
K E D A K S I E F O J Q B C M H F Q
K W A C K L N A B R L Y N A L X Q C
H T M R Y T G S M Y N L Y N C N F O
B K P F T M O K U R C H E A P E R G
H Q R C L P X M S N T H E R B L I G
L Y A G N N N M J T D Y F I S K J I
M J H F O P P J R L T A B E W B A N
K O T T V O C L F G A W Y S M X N H
G L R V C O U N C I L N H T A B E L
Q U A S F R B N G G S S G I X P R M
B T M F E G R D R V I B U U S G O M
S O I W N N Q O F L W I O V A T V T
H N F I A N S W O Z Z L C L I G L D
O S K M B I S O B T A L L O I A E E
E I B Z E K F Z D V G N N M N L G G
Y L W V M E R N E S T I N E O J L J
Z S E L S A E M D X Y Q R E J A Z Z
```

A unit of motion or thought (8)
All the children got the whooping ____ on the way home from CA (5)
At the ___ party the kids got tired of being angels & jumped into the sprinkler water (3)
Co-author; _____ Gilbreth Carey (9)
Dad did not like the ___ Age (4)
Dad had a bad one (5)
Dad's occupation; ___ study (6)
Dad's saying; By ____ (5)
Doctor who got Ernestine and Martha mixed up (6)
Father painted messages on the walls in ___ code (5)
Father put red ink spots on his face, pretending to have ___ (7)
He forgot to take the lens cap off the camera, so there were no movies of the tonsillectomy (6)
He looked like what might happen if a pygmy married a barber pole (3)
He made Aunt Anne furious by pretending to be a dog (4)
It terrified the children when Father took pictures (5)
Motorcycle ___ was caught peeping in Ernestine's window (3)
Name for the cottage (4)
Over the hill and to the ___ house (4)
Peter and Maggie (8)
She bobbed her hair (4)
She had power over Mother; Mother obeyed her (6)
She learned to do math quickly in her head (6)
She tried to organize a group of women to be advocates of birth control (6)
She underbid the others & painted the fence (4)
Signal for everyone to gather (7)
The bird ___ was Dad's only failure (4)
The boat (4)
The car; ____ Carriage (7)
The children and Dad had theirs removed (7)
The children buried one full of pencils (6)
The children studied recorded ____ lessons (8)
The children thought the Mollers were the kissingest ___ in the world (3)
The children went to ___ school because Mr. Gilbreth wanted them to have a well-rounded education (6
The family ___ was set up as a forum for making decisions & voicing grievances (7)
The last baby (4)
They were Mother's family (7)
____ By The Dozen (7)

Cheaper By The Dozen Word Search 1 Answer Key

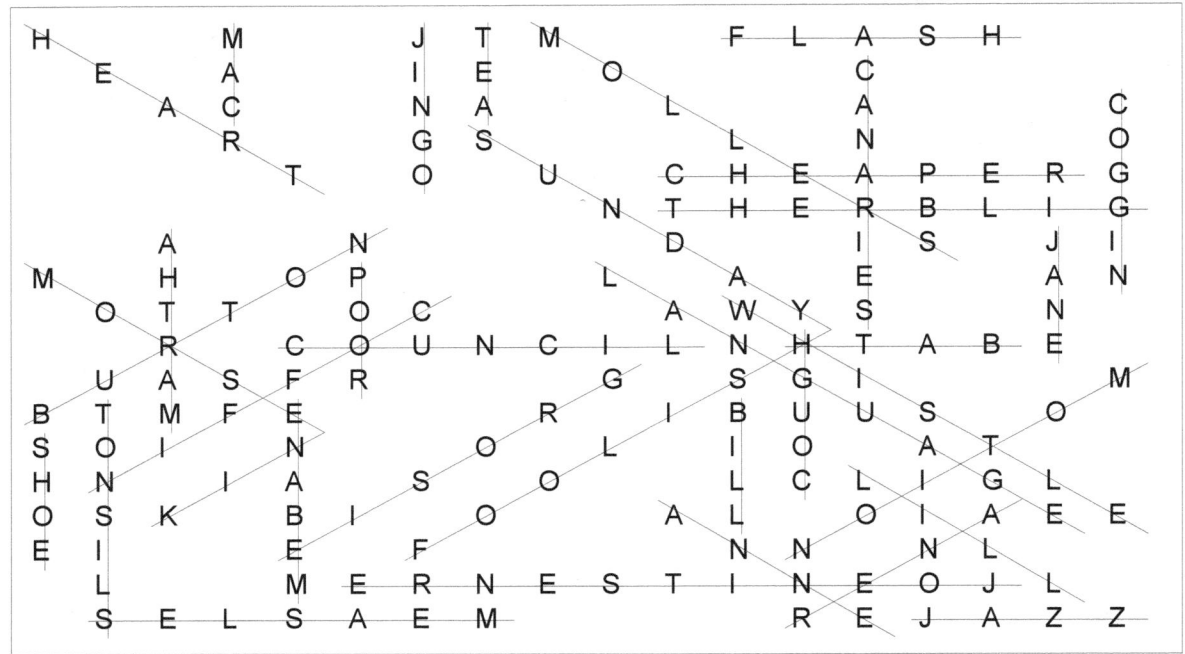

A unit of motion or thought (8)
All the children got the whooping ____ on the way home from CA (5)
At the ___ party the kids got tired of being angels & jumped into the sprinkler water (3)
Co-author; _____ Gilbreth Carey (9)
Dad did not like the ___ Age (4)
Dad had a bad one (5)
Dad's occupation; ___ study (6)
Dad's saying; By ____ (5)
Doctor who got Ernestine and Martha mixed up (6)
Father painted messages on the walls in ___ code (5)
Father put red ink spots on his face, pretending to have ___ (7)
He forgot to take the lens cap off the camera, so there were no movies of the tonsillectomy (6)
He looked like what might happen if a pygmy married a barber pole (3)
He made Aunt Anne furious by pretending to be a dog (4)
It terrified the children when Father took pictures (5)
Motorcycle ___ was caught peeping in Ernestine's window (3)
Name for the cottage (4)

Over the hill and to the ___ house (4)
Peter and Maggie (8)
She bobbed her hair (4)
She had power over Mother; Mother obeyed her (6)
She learned to do math quickly in her head (6)
She tried to organize a group of women to be advocates of birth control (6)
She underbid the others & painted the fence (4)
Signal for everyone to gather (7)
The bird ___ was Dad's only failure (4)
The boat (4)
The car; ____ Carriage (7)
The children and Dad had theirs removed (7)
The children buried one full of pencils (6)
The children studied recorded ____ lessons (8)
The children thought the Mollers were the kissingest ___ in the world (3)
The children went to ___ school because Mr. Gilbreth wanted them to have a well-rounded education (6)
The family ___ was set up as a forum for making decisions & voicing grievances (7)
The last baby (4)
They were Mother's family (7)
____ By The Dozen (7)

Cheaper By The Dozen Word Search 2

```
S P F R Y R H K I N R Z M E B A N E
E N O E V E Q P I E K Y I F S M D K
L Y N O Q N H G T F K S E F H O J S
S N Q Q R A G I T L O M I O R J Z
A T E A H O R C C R H A T C E S I W
E G H G C W X A G D S R S I C E N L
M B U T E S N L M H I T E B M G N
R O I P V A I I O C L H H N W A O K
C K Y L R R F F L Y O A W C N I T F
F T F I L T F O L H O U V Y T H E H
J T E J S T O R E M F X N O Z N S T
S S J A N E C N R J A C M C I R S R
D U L Z D G J I S G P C H T I L Z Q
V L N Z N H O A R G M N S E I L H D
S Z H D L V E N F V K E S S A F G F
Q F Y L A B Q A H Q N S N Q N P C T
T V I V Z Y C D R R H O T J Z N E R
M L B U R T O N E T T V S Z P F M R
```

All the children got the whooping _____ on the way home from CA (5)
At the ___ party the kids got tired of being angels & jumped into the sprinkler water (3)
Co-author; _____ Gilbreth Carey (9)
Dad did not like the ___ Age (4)
Dad had a bad one (5)
Dad was an _____ expert (10)
Dad's occupation; ___ study (6)
Dad's saying; By _____ (5)
Doctor who got Ernestine and Martha mixed up (6)
Father painted messages on the walls in ___ code (5)
Father put red ink spots on his face, pretending to have ___ (7)
He forgot to take the lens cap off the camera, so there were no movies of the tonsillectomy (6)
He looked like what might happen if a pygmy married a barber pole (3)
He made Aunt Anne furious by pretending to be a dog (4)
It terrified the children when Father took pictures (5)
It was named Moby Dick (10)
Motorcycle ___ was caught peeping in Ernestine's window (3)

Name for the cottage (4)
Over the hill and to the ___ house (4)
Peter and Maggie (8)
She bobbed her hair (4)
She had power over Mother; Mother obeyed her (6)
She learned to do math quickly in her head (6)
She tried to organize a group of women to be advocates of birth control (6)
She underbid the others & painted the fence (4)
Signal for everyone to gather (7)
State where Mollers lived (10)
The bird ___ was Dad's only failure (4)
The boat (4)
The car; _____ Carriage (7)
The children and Dad had theirs removed (7)
The children buried one full of pencils (6)
The children thought the Mollers were the kissingest ___ in the world (3)
The children went to ___ school because Mr. Gilbreth wanted them to have a well-rounded education (6)
The family ___ was set up as a forum for making decisions & voicing grievances (7)
The last baby (4)
They were Mother's family (7)
_____ By The Dozen (7)

Cheaper By The Dozen Word Search 2 Answer Key

All the children got the whooping ____ on the way home from CA (5)
At the ___ party the kids got tired of being angels & jumped into the sprinkler water (3)
Co-author; _____ Gilbreth Carey (9)
Dad did not like the ___ Age (4)
Dad had a bad one (5)
Dad was an ____ expert (10)
Dad's occupation; ___ study (6)
Dad's saying; By _____ (5)
Doctor who got Ernestine and Martha mixed up (6)
Father painted messages on the walls in ___ code (5)
Father put red ink spots on his face, pretending to have ___ (7)
He forgot to take the lens cap off the camera, so there were no movies of the tonsillectomy (6)
He looked like what might happen if a pygmy married a barber pole (3)
He made Aunt Anne furious by pretending to be a dog (4)
It terrified the children when Father took pictures (5)
It was named Moby Dick (10)
Motorcycle ___ was caught peeping in Ernestine's window (3)

Name for the cottage (4)
Over the hill and to the ___ house (4)
Peter and Maggie (8)
She bobbed her hair (4)
She had power over Mother; Mother obeyed her (6)
She learned to do math quickly in her head (6)
She tried to organize a group of women to be advocates of birth control (6)
She underbid the others & painted the fence (4)
Signal for everyone to gather (7)
State where Mollers lived (10)
The bird ___ was Dad's only failure (4)
The boat (4)
The car; _____ Carriage (7)
The children and Dad had theirs removed (7)
The children buried one full of pencils (6)
The children thought the Mollers were the kissingest ___ in the world (3)
The children went to ___ school because Mr. Gilbreth wanted them to have a well-rounded education (6)
The family ___ was set up as a forum for making decisions & voicing grievances (7)
The last baby (4)
They were Mother's family (7)
____ By The Dozen (7)

Cheaper By The Dozen Word Search 3

```
B R B Z S Q R C V T L S J K K S P C G J
R F X Z W L C Y J O H S X H L K T H R P
I F C L M M O Q I N X E N C J G K E O S
C T L P E D U Q N S J M A P B A N A S R
K I R A A D N L G I O R H R A O N P I V
L L P P S Y C H O L O G I S T J O E E W
A Z V H L H I O L S U R C R H F S R F H
Y V O R E D L E G O L H U N T R R N O W
E E J Q S Q R S C G L B I R O S M E O Z
R O O P W S B L Z B I K V M E T Y S L Q
E K C W R P J Z A F B N J I N Y T I Z
T T H R W F A M Q N R C R T A P A I S F
I E Q J H J X W A W G A T L B N D N H R
R A W F I M C Z T C N U M D E S N E D M
W P C T S A Y Y Y A I G A O M J U E Z G
E X C Y T R Z F C S F S F G T W S J W B
P R R F L T Z L S B F F G M E I D P M V
Y B K L E H M Y D V O R B G F F O F Q Y
T G T T F A E F F I C I E N C Y T N X R
C A L I F O R N I A T H E R B L I G C V
```

ANNE	COUNCIL	KIN	PSYCHOLOGIST
BATH	EFFICIENCY	LANGUAGE	RENA
BILL	ERNESTINE	LILL	SHOE
BRICKLAYER	FLASH	MAC	SUNDAY
BURTON	FOOLISH	MARTHA	TEA
CALIFORNIA	GROSIE	MEASLES	THERBLIG
CANARIES	HEART	MEBANE	TONSILS
CHEAPER	JANE	MOLLERS	TYPEWRITER
COFFIN	JAZZ	MORSE	WHISTLE
COGGIN	JINGO	MOTION	
COUGH	JOE	POOR	

Cheaper By The Dozen Word Search 3 Answer Key

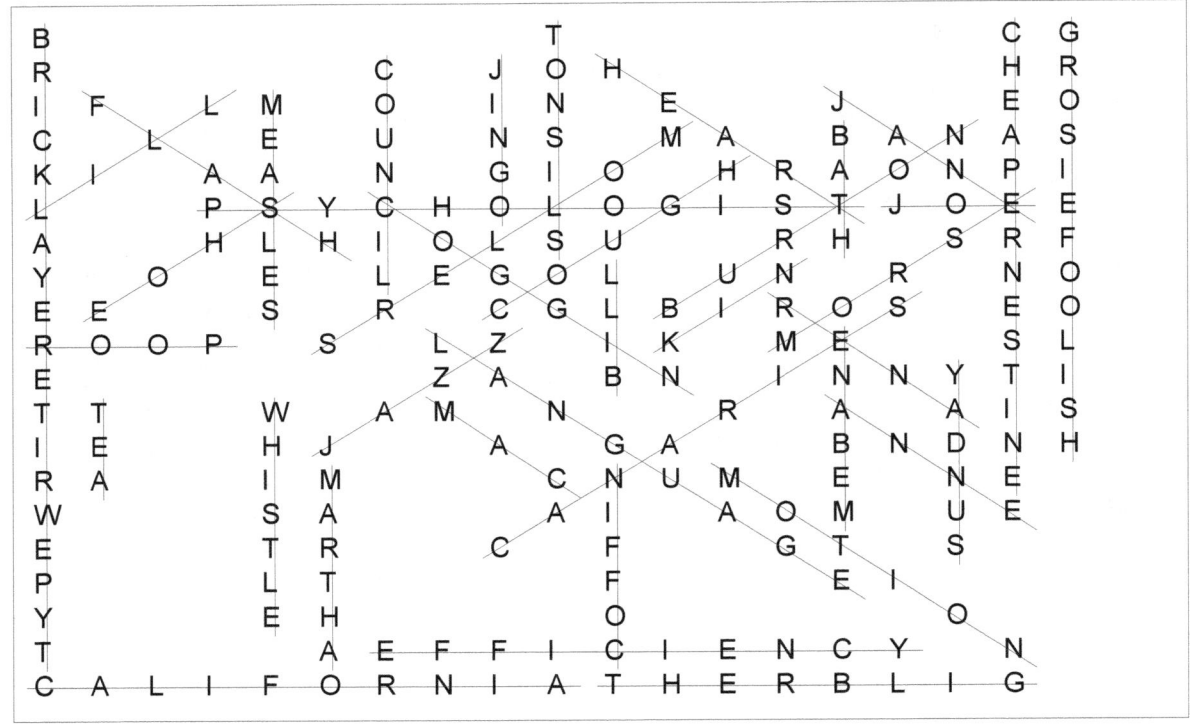

ANNE	COUNCIL	KIN	PSYCHOLOGIST
BATH	EFFICIENCY	LANGUAGE	RENA
BILL	ERNESTINE	LILL	SHOE
BRICKLAYER	FLASH	MAC	SUNDAY
BURTON	FOOLISH	MARTHA	TEA
CALIFORNIA	GROSIE	MEASLES	THERBLIG
CANARIES	HEART	MEBANE	TONSILS
CHEAPER	JANE	MOLLERS	TYPEWRITER
COFFIN	JAZZ	MORSE	WHISTLE
COGGIN	JINGO	MOTION	
COUGH	JOE	POOR	

Cheaper By The Dozen Word Search 4

```
J K S M X V M J Z C S W P R S Q J K Y G
M A U G M S G O F S O T X O H R F L C R
A N N E R L I L M D G F O O L I S H J
C X D E M O T I A L A N G B E R W E E F
Y Y A Q C E S B S B E R T I N R A B A K
K L Y M O N A I H W U R T T N R E I P M
B I M J O N Y S E S H R S H T J R L E X
R C N T E R V D L T L I T G A I N L R B
I N B R C Z S M Z E G L S O X N E T C Z
C U M A Q V T E A O S A W T N G S Y O C
K O Q Q T V B L L T G N Q V L O T P U T
L C F W J H S O S H K G K E H E I E G D
A Q H F F G H G R B X U N N T P N W H S
Y C N E I C I F F E H A J L Z G E R E L
E H P S Y N C Z C Z B G C Z Y K S I X V
R F N S P X K D D E C A S G B R T X R
G S P B H L K K M R X J V M Z A Z E J S
M O T I O N T H E R B L I G N S S R C R
Q C H M N H T T M F F J Y A W Y G Y H N
C A L I F O R N I A P Q C N S Y H S N B
```

ANNE	COUNCIL	KIN	PSYCHOLOGIST
BATH	EFFICIENCY	LANGUAGE	RENA
BILL	ERNESTINE	LILL	SHOE
BRICKLAYER	FLASH	MAC	SUNDAY
BURTON	FOOLISH	MARTHA	TEA
CALIFORNIA	GROSIE	MEASLES	THERBLIG
CANARIES	HEART	MEBANE	TONSILS
CHEAPER	JANE	MOLLERS	TYPEWRITER
COFFIN	JAZZ	MORSE	WHISTLE
COGGIN	JINGO	MOTION	
COUGH	JOE	POOR	

Cheaper By The Dozen Word Search 4 Answer Key

ANNE	COUNCIL	KIN	PSYCHOLOGIST
BATH	EFFICIENCY	LANGUAGE	RENA
BILL	ERNESTINE	LILL	SHOE
BRICKLAYER	FLASH	MAC	SUNDAY
BURTON	FOOLISH	MARTHA	TEA
CALIFORNIA	GROSIE	MEASLES	THERBLIG
CANARIES	HEART	MEBANE	TONSILS
CHEAPER	JANE	MOLLERS	TYPEWRITER
COFFIN	JAZZ	MORSE	WHISTLE
COGGIN	JINGO	MOTION	
COUGH	JOE	POOR	

Cheaper By The Dozen Crossword 1

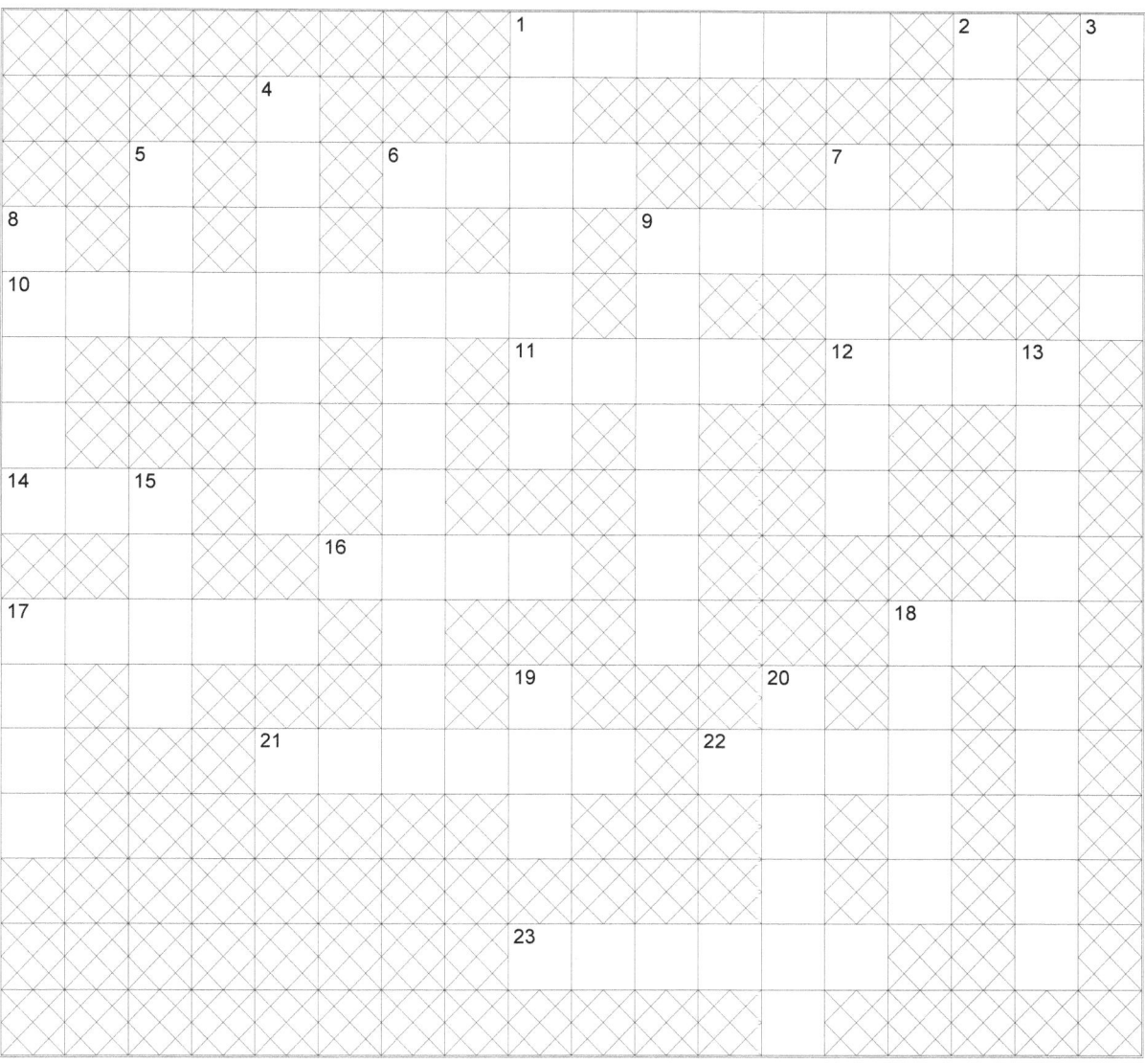

Across
1. Dad's occupation; ___ study
6. He made Aunt Anne furious by pretending to be a dog
9. A unit of motion or thought
10. Co-author; _____ Gilbreth Carey
11. The boat
12. Name for the cottage
14. At the ___ party the kids got tired of being angels & jumped into the sprinkler water
16. The bird ___ was Dad's only failure
17. Dad's saying; By ____
18. Motorcycle ___ was caught peeping in Ernestine's window
21. Doctor who got Ernestine and Martha mixed up
22. Over the hill and to the ___ house
23. He forgot to take the lens cap off the camera, so there were no movies of the tonsillectomy

Down
1. They were Mother's family
2. She underbid the others & painted the fence
3. All the children got the whooping ____ on the way home from CA
4. Signal for everyone to gather
5. The children thought the Mollers were the kissingest ___ in the world
6. Father began work as a _____'s helper
7. She had power over Mother; Mother obeyed her
8. Dad had a bad one
9. The children and Dad had theirs removed
13. Dad was an ____ expert
15. She bobbed her hair
17. Dad did not like the ___ Age
18. Father painted messages on the walls in ___ code
19. He looked like what might happen if a pygmy married a barber pole
20. The children buried one full of pencils

Cheaper By The Dozen Crossword 1 Answer Key

						¹M	O	T	I	O	N		²L		³C
			⁴W			O							I		O
		⁵K		⁶H		B	I	L	L		⁷G		L		U
⁸H	I	I	R			L		⁹T	H	E	R	B	L	I	G
¹⁰E	R	N	E	S	T	I	N	E			O		O		H
A		T		C		¹¹R	E	N	A		¹²S	H	O	¹³E	
R		L		K		S		S			I			F	
¹⁴T	¹⁵E	A		E	L			I			E			F	
	N			¹⁶B	A	T	H							I	
¹⁷J	I	N	G	O		Y		L					¹⁸M	A	C
A		E				E		¹⁹J		²⁰C		O		I
Z			²¹B	U	R	T	O	N		²²P	O	O	R		E
Z						E				F			S		N
										F			E		C
						²³C	O	G	G	I	N				Y
										N					

Across
1. Dad's occupation; ___ study
6. He made Aunt Anne furious by pretending to be a dog
9. A unit of motion or thought
10. Co-author; _____ Gilbreth Carey
11. The boat
12. Name for the cottage
14. At the ___ party the kids got tired of being angels & jumped into the sprinkler water
16. The bird ___ was Dad's only failure
17. Dad's saying; By ____
18. Motorcycle ___ was caught peeping in Ernestine's window
21. Doctor who got Ernestine and Martha mixed up
22. Over the hill and to the ___ house
23. He forgot to take the lens cap off the camera, so there were no movies of the tonsillectomy

Down
1. They were Mother's family
2. She underbid the others & painted the fence
3. All the children got the whooping ____ on the way home from CA
4. Signal for everyone to gather
5. The children thought the Mollers were the kissingest ___ in the world
6. Father began work as a _____'s helper
7. She had power over Mother; Mother obeyed her
8. Dad had a bad one
9. The children and Dad had theirs removed
13. Dad was an ____ expert
15. She bobbed her hair
17. Dad did not like the ___ Age
18. Father painted messages on the walls in ___ code
19. He looked like what might happen if a pygmy married a barber pole
20. The children buried one full of pencils

Cheaper By The Dozen Crossword 2

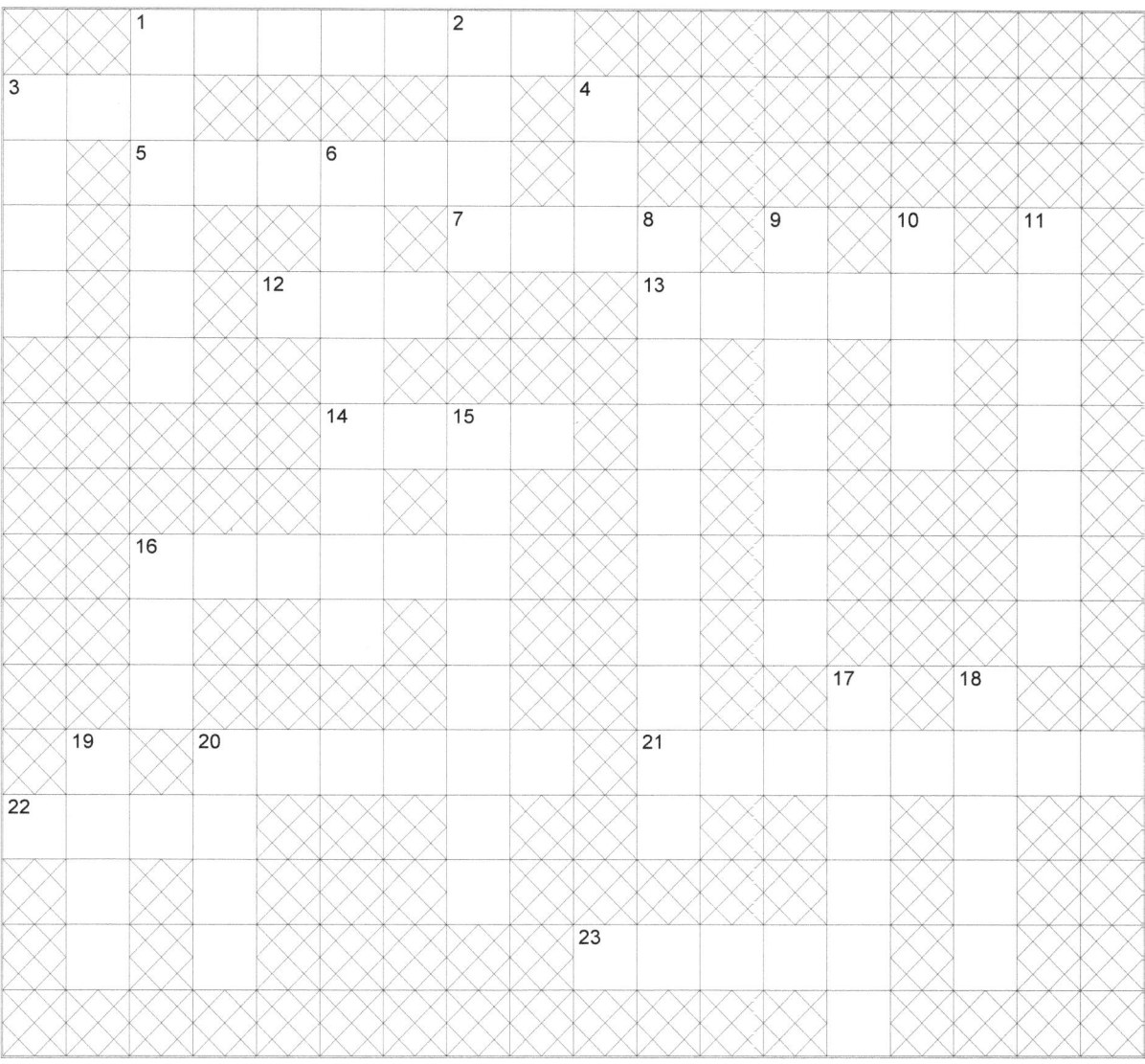

Across
1. They were Mother's family
3. He looked like what might happen if a pygmy married a barber pole
5. Doctor who got Ernestine and Martha mixed up
7. She bobbed her hair
12. At the ___ party the kids got tired of being angels & jumped into the sprinkler water
13. The car; ____ Carriage
14. He made Aunt Anne furious by pretending to be a dog
16. Dad's occupation; ___ study
20. The children went to ___ school because Mr. Gilbreth wanted them to have a well-rounded education
21. Peter and Maggie
22. The bird ___ was Dad's only failure
23. It terrified the children when Father took pictures

Down
1. She tried to organize a group of women to be advocates of birth control
2. The boat
3. The last baby
4. The children thought the Mollers were the kissingest ___ in the world
6. A unit of motion or thought
8. Dad was an ____ expert
9. The family ___ was set up as a forum for making decisions & voicing grievances
10. She underbid the others & painted the fence
11. Signal for everyone to gather
15. The children studied recorded ____ lessons
16. Motorcycle ___ was caught peeping in Ernestine's window
17. She learned to do math quickly in her head
18. Dad's saying; By ____
19. Dad did not like the ___ Age
20. Name for the cottage

Cheaper By The Dozen Crossword 2 Answer Key

		1 M	O	L	L	2 R	S				
3 J	O	E				E		4 K			
A		5 B	U	6 R	T	O	N	I			
N		A		H		7 A	N	8 N	9 C	10 L	11 W
E		N		12 T	E	A		13 F	O	O	L	I	S	H
		E		R				F	U	L		I
				14 B	I	15 L	L		I	N		L	S
				L		A			C	C		T
		16 M	O	T	I	O	N		I	I		L
		A				G		G		E	L		
		C						U		N	17 M	18 J
	19 J	20 S	U	N	D	A	Y		21 C	A	N	A	R	I	E	S
22 B	A	T	H			G			Y		R		N
		Z	O			E					T		G
		Z	E				23 F	L	A	S	H		O
							A					

Across
1. They were Mother's family
3. He looked like what might happen if a pygmy married a barber pole
5. Doctor who got Ernestine and Martha mixed up
7. She bobbed her hair
12. At the ___ party the kids got tired of being angels & jumped into the sprinkler water
13. The car; ____ Carriage
14. He made Aunt Anne furious by pretending to be a dog
16. Dad's occupation; ___ study
20. The children went to ___ school because Mr. Gilbreth wanted them to have a well-rounded education
21. Peter and Maggie
22. The bird ___ was Dad's only failure
23. It terrified the children when Father took pictures

Down
1. She tried to organize a group of women to be advocates of birth control
2. The boat
3. The last baby
4. The children thought the Mollers were the kissingest ___ in the world
6. A unit of motion or thought
8. Dad was an ____ expert
9. The family ___ was set up as a forum for making decisions & voicing grievances
10. She underbid the others & painted the fence
11. Signal for everyone to gather
15. The children studied recorded ____ lessons
16. Motorcycle ___ was caught peeping in Ernestine's window
17. She learned to do math quickly in her head
18. Dad's saying; By ____
19. Dad did not like the ___ Age
20. Name for the cottage

Cheaper By The Dozen Cossword 3

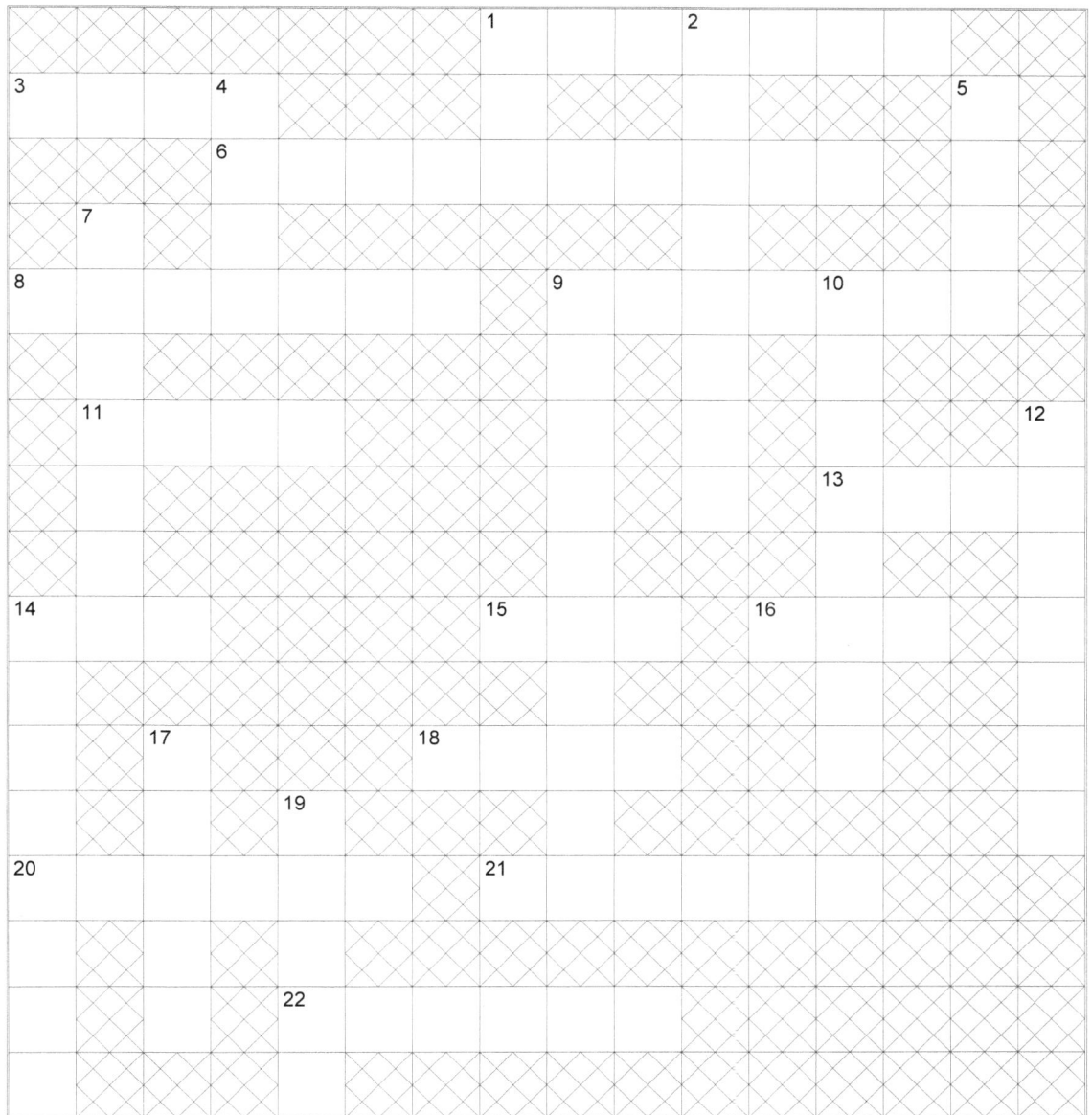

Across
1. They were Mother's family
3. Over the hill and to the ___ house
6. Dad was an ___ expert
8. ___ By The Dozen
9. The family ___ was set up as a forum for making decisions & voicing grievances
11. Name for the cottage
13. She bobbed her hair
14. At the ___ party the kids got tired of being angels & jumped into the sprinkler water
15. He looked like what might happen if a pygmy married a barber pole
16. The children thought the Mollers were the kissingest ___ in the world
18. The last baby
20. Doctor who got Ernestine and Martha mixed up
21. She learned to do math quickly in her head
22. She had power over Mother; Mother obeyed her

Down
1. Motorcycle ___ was caught peeping in Ernestine's window
2. The children studied recorded ___ lessons
4. The boat
5. She underbid the others & painted the fence
7. Signal for everyone to gather
9. State where Mollers lived
10. Peter and Maggie
12. Father put red ink spots on his face, pretending to have ___
14. A unit of motion or thought
17. Father painted messages on the walls in ___ code
19. All the children got the whooping ___ on the way home from CA

Cheaper By The Dozen Crossword 3 Answer Key

					¹M	O	L	²L	E	R	S	
³P	O	O	⁴R		A			A			⁵L	
			⁶E	F	F	I	C	I	E	N	C	Y
	⁷W		N					G			L	
⁸C	H	E	A	P	E	R		⁹C	O	U	¹⁰N	C	I	L
	I							A			A	
	¹¹S	H	O	E				L			N		¹²M
	T							I			¹³A	N	N	E
	L							F			R		A
¹⁴T	E	A				¹⁵J	O	E		¹⁶K	I	N	S
H						R				E			L
E		¹⁷M			¹⁸J	A	N	E		S			E
R		O		¹⁹C		I				S			S
²⁰B	U	R	T	O	N		²¹M	A	R	T	H	A
L		S		U								
I		E		²²G	R	O	S	I	E			
G				H								

Across
1. They were Mother's family
3. Over the hill and to the ___ house
6. Dad was an ____ expert
8. ____ By The Dozen
9. The family ___ was set up as a forum for making decisions & voicing grievances
11. Name for the cottage
13. She bobbed her hair
14. At the ___ party the kids got tired of being angels & jumped into the sprinkler water
15. He looked like what might happen if a pygmy married a barber pole
16. The children thought the Mollers were the kissingest ___ in the world
18. The last baby
20. Doctor who got Ernestine and Martha mixed up
21. She learned to do math quickly in her head
22. She had power over Mother; Mother obeyed her

Down
1. Motorcycle ___ was caught peeping in Ernestine's window
2. The children studied recorded ____ lessons
4. The boat
5. She underbid the others & painted the fence
7. Signal for everyone to gather
9. State where Mollers lived
10. Peter and Maggie
12. Father put red ink spots on his face, pretending to have ___
14. A unit of motion or thought
17. Father painted messages on the walls in ___ code
19. All the children got the whooping ____ on the way home from CA

Cheaper By The Dozen Crossword 4

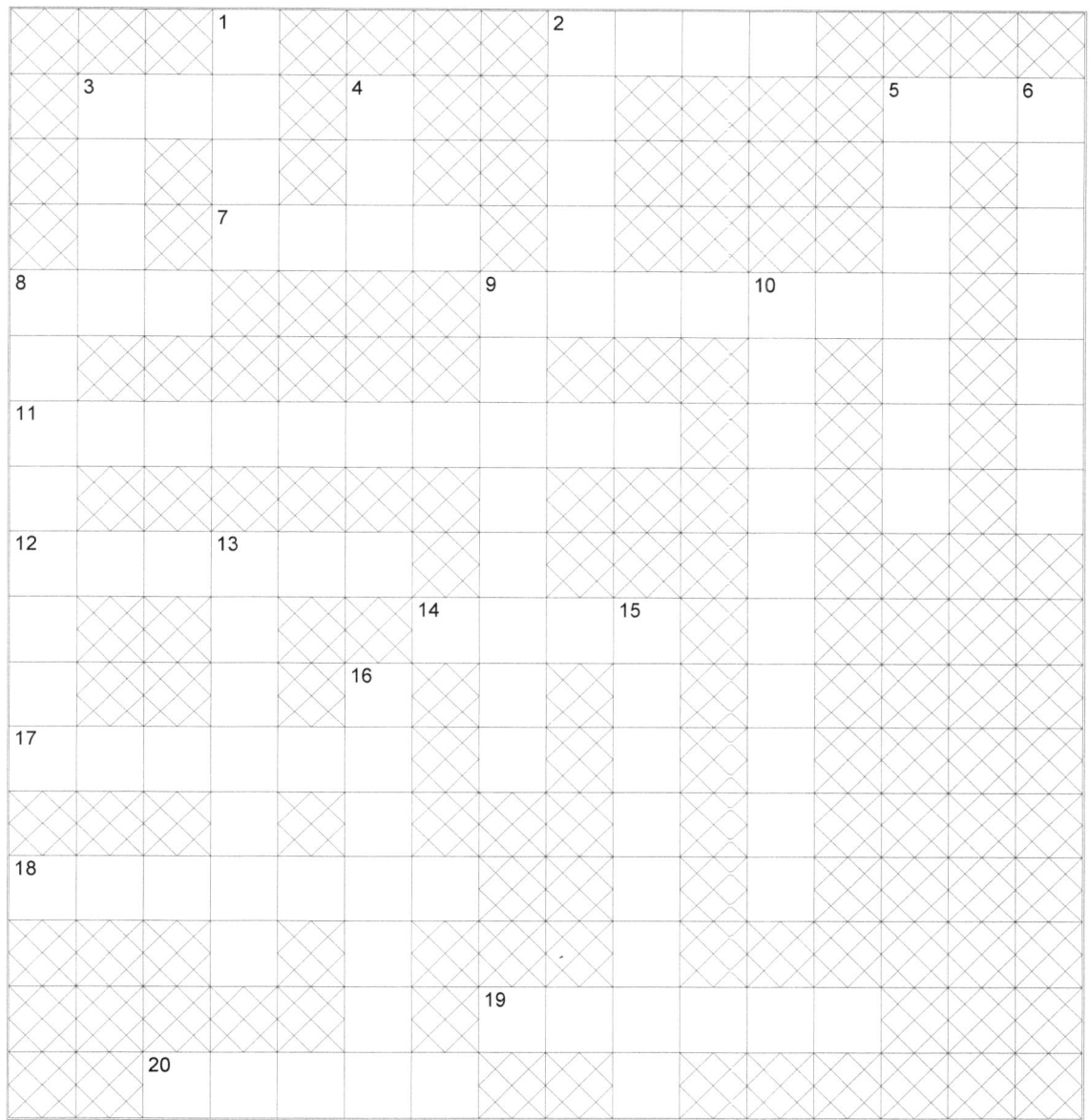

Across
2. Dad did not like the ___ Age
3. He looked like what might happen if a pygmy married a barber pole
5. Motorcycle ___ was caught peeping in Ernestine's window
7. She bobbed her hair
8. At the ___ party the kids got tired of being angels & jumped into the sprinkler water
9. The family ___ was set up as a forum for making decisions & voicing grievances
11. Dad was an ___ expert
12. Doctor who got Ernestine and Martha mixed up
14. She underbid the others & painted the fence
17. She had power over Mother; Mother obeyed her
18. The car; ___ Carriage
19. He forgot to take the lens cap off the camera, so there were no movies of the tonsillectomy
20. Father painted messages on the walls in ___ code

Down
1. The boat
2. Dad's saying; By ___
3. The last baby
4. The children thought the Mollers were the kissingest ___ in the world
5. They were Mother's family
6. ___ By The Dozen
8. A unit of motion or thought
9. Peter and Maggie
10. State where Mollers lived
13. The children and Dad had theirs removed
15. The children studied recorded ___ lessons
16. Father put red ink spots on his face, pretending to have ___

Cheaper By The Dozen Crossword 4 Answer Key

		1 R			2 J	A	Z	Z		
	3 J	O	E	4 K		I			5 M	A C 6
		A		N		N			O	H
		N		7 A	N N	E			L	E
8 T	E	A				9 C	O	U	10 N C	I L A
H						A			C	A E P
11 E	F	F	I	C	I	E	N	C	Y	L R E
R						A				I S R
12 B	U	R	13 T	O	N		R			F
L			O			14 L	I	15 L		O
I			N		16 M	E	A	S		R
17 G	R	O	S	I	E		S		N	N
			I		A				G	I
18 F	O	O	L	I	S	H			U	A
			S		L				A	
			E		19 C	O	G	G	I	N
	20 M	O	R	S	E				E	

Across
2. Dad did not like the ___ Age
3. He looked like what might happen if a pygmy married a barber pole
5. Motorcycle ___ was caught peeping in Ernestine's window
7. She bobbed her hair
8. At the ___ party the kids got tired of being angels & jumped into the sprinkler water
9. The family ___ was set up as a forum for making decisions & voicing grievances
11. Dad was an ____ expert
12. Doctor who got Ernestine and Martha mixed up
14. She underbid the others & painted the fence
17. She had power over Mother; Mother obeyed her
18. The car; ____ Carriage
19. He forgot to take the lens cap off the camera, so there were no movies of the tonsillectomy
20. Father painted messages on the walls in ___ code

Down
1. The boat
2. Dad's saying; By ____
3. The last baby
4. The children thought the Mollers were the kissingest ___ in the world
5. They were Mother's family
6. ____ By The Dozen
8. A unit of motion or thought
9. Peter and Maggie
10. State where Mollers lived
13. The children and Dad had theirs removed
15. The children studied recorded ____ lessons
16. Father put red ink spots on his face, pretending to have ___

Cheaper By The Dozen

TEA	THERBLIG	BATH	COFFIN	ANNE
PSYCHOLOGIST	MOTION	CHEAPER	KIN	MAC
MARTHA	MEBANE	FREE SPACE	BRICKLAYER	RENA
JINGO	COUGH	WHISTLE	FOOLISH	LANGUAGE
MORSE	FLASH	COUNCIL	TONSILS	MEASLES

Cheaper By The Dozen

JAZZ	SUNDAY	CALIFORNIA	JANE	GROSIE
TYPEWRITER	COGGIN	MOLLERS	HEART	BURTON
ERNESTINE	EFFICIENCY	FREE SPACE	CANARIES	SHOE
BILL	JOE	MEASLES	TONSILS	COUNCIL
FLASH	MORSE	LANGUAGE	FOOLISH	WHISTLE

Cheaper By The Dozen

ANNE	JANE	JAZZ	COGGIN	GROSIE
FLASH	COUNCIL	RENA	SUNDAY	FOOLISH
JINGO	JOE	FREE SPACE	SHOE	TYPEWRITER
MOLLERS	MARTHA	MAC	COFFIN	BURTON
MOTION	LILL	TEA	MEBANE	MEASLES

Cheaper By The Dozen

CALIFORNIA	PSYCHOLOGIST	HEART	WHISTLE	BRICKLAYER
BILL	THERBLIG	CHEAPER	KIN	CANARIES
EFFICIENCY	LANGUAGE	FREE SPACE	TONSILS	ERNESTINE
MORSE	BATH	MEASLES	MEBANE	TEA
LILL	MOTION	BURTON	COFFIN	MAC

Cheaper By The Dozen

GROSIE	SUNDAY	MOTION	LANGUAGE	MARTHA
FLASH	COGGIN	TYPEWRITER	BATH	THERBLIG
COUNCIL	KIN	FREE SPACE	TONSILS	ANNE
FOOLISH	COFFIN	MEBANE	ERNESTINE	MEASLES
JOE	COUGH	HEART	WHISTLE	MOLLERS

Cheaper By The Dozen

EFFICIENCY	BURTON	JAZZ	LILL	POOR
BRICKLAYER	TEA	CALIFORNIA	PSYCHOLOGIST	BILL
JINGO	SHOE	FREE SPACE	MAC	JANE
CHEAPER	CANARIES	MOLLERS	WHISTLE	HEART
COUGH	JOE	MEASLES	ERNESTINE	MEBANE

Cheaper By The Dozen

JAZZ	ERNESTINE	ANNE	SUNDAY	MOLLERS
COUNCIL	THERBLIG	MEASLES	FLASH	TEA
COGGIN	MAC	FREE SPACE	TONSILS	FOOLISH
GROSIE	CALIFORNIA	BURTON	MOTION	BRICKLAYER
WHISTLE	BATH	POOR	CANARIES	SHOE

Cheaper By The Dozen

EFFICIENCY	CHEAPER	MARTHA	COUGH	TYPEWRITER
JINGO	BILL	KIN	HEART	MEBANE
LILL	JOE	FREE SPACE	PSYCHOLOGIST	COFFIN
RENA	MORSE	SHOE	CANARIES	POOR
BATH	WHISTLE	BRICKLAYER	MOTION	BURTON

Cheaper By The Dozen

EFFICIENCY	ANNE	TONSILS	TYPEWRITER	CALIFORNIA
COUGH	LANGUAGE	JANE	LILL	BRICKLAYER
THERBLIG	COUNCIL	FREE SPACE	BURTON	CANARIES
COGGIN	WHISTLE	JOE	MORSE	MOTION
MAC	SUNDAY	BILL	CHEAPER	JAZZ

Cheaper By The Dozen

POOR	ERNESTINE	MARTHA	BATH	KIN
SHOE	MEBANE	JINGO	FLASH	MEASLES
TEA	PSYCHOLOGIST	FREE SPACE	HEART	COFFIN
RENA	MOLLERS	JAZZ	CHEAPER	BILL
SUNDAY	MAC	MOTION	MORSE	JOE

Cheaper By The Dozen

COUGH	RENA	MOTION	MEBANE	WHISTLE
TONSILS	JANE	POOR	HEART	MAC
THERBLIG	MOLLERS	FREE SPACE	LILL	FOOLISH
MARTHA	CANARIES	COGGIN	ANNE	ERNESTINE
SHOE	BILL	JOE	BRICKLAYER	LANGUAGE

Cheaper By The Dozen

CHEAPER	TEA	KIN	TYPEWRITER	GROSIE
JAZZ	BATH	FLASH	CALIFORNIA	PSYCHOLOGIST
JINGO	EFFICIENCY	FREE SPACE	SUNDAY	MEASLES
COUNCIL	COFFIN	LANGUAGE	BRICKLAYER	JOE
BILL	SHOE	ERNESTINE	ANNE	COGGIN

Cheaper By The Dozen

MEBANE	BILL	EFFICIENCY	COGGIN	SHOE
CHEAPER	WHISTLE	LANGUAGE	MEASLES	JINGO
PSYCHOLOGIST	MARTHA	FREE SPACE	FLASH	BURTON
COUNCIL	SUNDAY	CALIFORNIA	FOOLISH	RENA
ERNESTINE	THERBLIG	HEART	BRICKLAYER	KIN

Cheaper By The Dozen

POOR	MOLLERS	ANNE	LILL	TONSILS
JAZZ	MORSE	TYPEWRITER	COFFIN	JANE
JOE	TEA	FREE SPACE	BATH	GROSIE
MOTION	MAC	KIN	BRICKLAYER	HEART
THERBLIG	ERNESTINE	RENA	FOOLISH	CALIFORNIA

Cheaper By The Dozen

TYPEWRITER	MOTION	RENA	EFFICIENCY	MEASLES
WHISTLE	LILL	MARTHA	JAZZ	MORSE
THERBLIG	TONSILS	FREE SPACE	MEBANE	CANARIES
ANNE	CHEAPER	CALIFORNIA	COUNCIL	ERNESTINE
PSYCHOLOGIST	TEA	SUNDAY	FOOLISH	POOR

Cheaper By The Dozen

SHOE	HEART	COGGIN	COUGH	FLASH
MOLLERS	BILL	BATH	JINGO	LANGUAGE
GROSIE	JOE	FREE SPACE	COFFIN	BRICKLAYER
JANE	KIN	POOR	FOOLISH	SUNDAY
TEA	PSYCHOLOGIST	ERNESTINE	COUNCIL	CALIFORNIA

Cheaper By The Dozen

POOR	COGGIN	CALIFORNIA	BATH	JOE
MEBANE	JINGO	KIN	CANARIES	MARTHA
BRICKLAYER	TYPEWRITER	FREE SPACE	JAZZ	ANNE
LILL	HEART	MOTION	PSYCHOLOGIST	SUNDAY
FOOLISH	MOLLERS	BILL	JANE	COUGH

Cheaper By The Dozen

MEASLES	THERBLIG	BURTON	RENA	TEA
GROSIE	WHISTLE	TONSILS	FLASH	MAC
MORSE	SHOE	FREE SPACE	CHEAPER	ERNESTINE
EFFICIENCY	COUNCIL	COUGH	JANE	BILL
MOLLERS	FOOLISH	SUNDAY	PSYCHOLOGIST	MOTION

Cheaper By The Dozen

WHISTLE	BURTON	MORSE	GROSIE	BATH
ERNESTINE	MAC	JOE	TEA	SUNDAY
PSYCHOLOGIST	COGGIN	FREE SPACE	POOR	CALIFORNIA
COUGH	HEART	BRICKLAYER	CANARIES	RENA
ANNE	SHOE	KIN	COFFIN	EFFICIENCY

Cheaper By The Dozen

CHEAPER	MOLLERS	MOTION	COUNCIL	MEBANE
FOOLISH	JAZZ	LANGUAGE	BILL	JINGO
JANE	MEASLES	FREE SPACE	TONSILS	MARTHA
LILL	FLASH	EFFICIENCY	COFFIN	KIN
SHOE	ANNE	RENA	CANARIES	BRICKLAYER

Cheaper By The Dozen

JAZZ	SUNDAY	HEART	BRICKLAYER	MEASLES
MARTHA	CALIFORNIA	LILL	JINGO	FOOLISH
CHEAPER	CANARIES	FREE SPACE	BILL	TEA
RENA	THERBLIG	FLASH	JANE	ERNESTINE
PSYCHOLOGIST	MAC	COGGIN	COUNCIL	MEBANE

Cheaper By The Dozen

SHOE	COFFIN	JOE	WHISTLE	TYPEWRITER
MOLLERS	GROSIE	ANNE	MORSE	LANGUAGE
BURTON	MOTION	FREE SPACE	COUGH	BATH
EFFICIENCY	KIN	MEBANE	COUNCIL	COGGIN
MAC	PSYCHOLOGIST	ERNESTINE	JANE	FLASH

Cheaper By The Dozen

MEASLES	MEBANE	LILL	POOR	SUNDAY
BATH	GROSIE	SHOE	ERNESTINE	LANGUAGE
COUGH	CHEAPER	FREE SPACE	CANARIES	PSYCHOLOGIST
FLASH	ANNE	FOOLISH	JINGO	COUNCIL
TONSILS	HEART	CALIFORNIA	EFFICIENCY	THERBLIG

Cheaper By The Dozen

TYPEWRITER	MOTION	BILL	JOE	KIN
BRICKLAYER	MAC	JANE	MORSE	MOLLERS
COFFIN	MARTHA	FREE SPACE	BURTON	WHISTLE
TEA	RENA	THERBLIG	EFFICIENCY	CALIFORNIA
HEART	TONSILS	COUNCIL	JINGO	FOOLISH

Cheaper By The Dozen

BILL	CALIFORNIA	COUGH	THERBLIG	COFFIN
COGGIN	GROSIE	MARTHA	MOTION	RENA
MOLLERS	PSYCHOLOGIST	FREE SPACE	JANE	JINGO
LANGUAGE	ANNE	SUNDAY	HEART	MEASLES
EFFICIENCY	TYPEWRITER	BATH	BURTON	JAZZ

Cheaper By The Dozen

JOE	SHOE	CANARIES	POOR	FOOLISH
TEA	COUNCIL	WHISTLE	BRICKLAYER	MEBANE
FLASH	MAC	FREE SPACE	KIN	TONSILS
LILL	ERNESTINE	JAZZ	BURTON	BATH
TYPEWRITER	EFFICIENCY	MEASLES	HEART	SUNDAY

Cheaper By The Dozen

PSYCHOLOGIST	GROSIE	MEBANE	LANGUAGE	THERBLIG
LILL	JOE	SUNDAY	SHOE	MAC
CALIFORNIA	POOR	FREE SPACE	BATH	COUGH
TYPEWRITER	FOOLISH	BRICKLAYER	CANARIES	BURTON
MEASLES	ERNESTINE	EFFICIENCY	KIN	TONSILS

Cheaper By The Dozen

JINGO	MORSE	WHISTLE	HEART	COFFIN
COGGIN	TEA	ANNE	BILL	FLASH
MARTHA	MOTION	FREE SPACE	COUNCIL	MOLLERS
CHEAPER	JAZZ	TONSILS	KIN	EFFICIENCY
ERNESTINE	MEASLES	BURTON	CANARIES	BRICKLAYER

Cheaper By The Dozen

COFFIN	POOR	MORSE	THERBLIG	LILL
COUNCIL	COUGH	SUNDAY	FOOLISH	RENA
MAC	EFFICIENCY	FREE SPACE	JANE	BILL
PSYCHOLOGIST	JOE	MARTHA	CANARIES	MEBANE
BURTON	BRICKLAYER	SHOE	COGGIN	FLASH

Cheaper By The Dozen

TEA	BATH	TONSILS	HEART	JAZZ
JINGO	KIN	ANNE	WHISTLE	GROSIE
TYPEWRITER	CALIFORNIA	FREE SPACE	CHEAPER	ERNESTINE
LANGUAGE	MEASLES	FLASH	COGGIN	SHOE
BRICKLAYER	BURTON	MEBANE	CANARIES	MARTHA

Cheaper By The Dozen

MOLLERS	JANE	THERBLIG	CANARIES	MEBANE
MEASLES	GROSIE	POOR	CHEAPER	COUGH
LILL	ERNESTINE	FREE SPACE	TEA	RENA
MORSE	ANNE	PSYCHOLOGIST	CALIFORNIA	COGGIN
BATH	COUNCIL	JAZZ	BRICKLAYER	LANGUAGE

Cheaper By The Dozen

MOTION	MAC	FOOLISH	JINGO	KIN
MARTHA	EFFICIENCY	SHOE	TYPEWRITER	BILL
JOE	COFFIN	FREE SPACE	WHISTLE	HEART
FLASH	SUNDAY	LANGUAGE	BRICKLAYER	JAZZ
COUNCIL	BATH	COGGIN	CALIFORNIA	PSYCHOLOGIST

Cheaper By The Dozen Vocabulary Word List Continued

No.	Word	Clue/Definition
1.	ADMONISHED	Kindly but seriously reprimanded
2.	AGENDA	List of things to be done
3.	AILING	Ill; sick
4.	ALIAS	An assumed name
5.	APPRECIATIVE	Grateful
6.	APTITUDE	Ability
7.	ASCERTAIN	Find out
8.	ATROCIOUS	Exceptionally bad
9.	AWE	An emotion of respect and wonder tinged with fear
10.	BEDLAM	Noisy uproar and confusion
11.	BELLIGERENT	Aggressive; hostile
12.	BENEVOLENT	Kind; charitable
13.	CALLIOPE	Musical keyboard fitted with steam whistles
14.	CAPITULATED	Yielded; gave in
15.	CAUCUS	A meeting to decide upon questions of policy
16.	COINCIDE	To happen at the same time
17.	CONCEDED	Admitted; acknowledged as true
18.	CONFERRED	Bestowed or given as an honor
19.	CONTAGIOUS	Tending to spread from one to another
20.	CONVENT	Home for nuns
21.	CONVERGED	Approached the same point from different directions
22.	CONVICTION	Strong belief
23.	DEBACLE	Disaster
24.	DEBUTANTE	Young woman who is formally presented to society
25.	DELECTABLE	Enjoyable; delightful
26.	DERELICTS	Social outcasts
27.	DETEST	Dislike intensely
28.	DILEMMA	A situation requiring a choice
29.	DIRE	Terrible; disastrous
30.	DOCILE	Obedient; submissive to management
31.	DORY	Small, narrow, flat-bottomed boat
32.	EMERGE	To come forth from; come into sight
33.	ENSCONCED	Settled securely
34.	ENSUE	To follow immediately after
35.	ENTAIL	To have a necessary accompaniment or consequences
36.	EXTRICATE	Release from entanglement
37.	FATALISTIC	Belief that events are predetermined; submission to fate
38.	FATIGUING	Tiring
39.	FEROCITY	Savage fierceness
40.	FORGO	Give up
41.	FRAUGHT	Accompanied by or filled with something undesirable
42.	GALL	Self-assertiveness
43.	IMPLIED	Suggested without directly saying
44.	IMPLORED	Begged for urgently
45.	INAUGURATED	Began
46.	INCENTIVE	A reward offered to motivate one to action
47.	INCREDULOUSLY	Expressing disbelief
48.	INDICATE	Demonstrate or point out
49.	INDIGNANTLY	Angrily because of something unjust
50.	INDOLENT	Lazy
51.	INEVITABLE	Unavoidable; going to happen no matter what

Cheaper By The Dozen Vocabulary Word List Continued

No.	Word	Clue/Definition
52.	INNOCUOUS	Harmless
53.	INNUENDOES	Things (usually negative) implied or suggested
54.	INTERVENE	To come between; interfere
55.	INTRICACIES	Many complexly arranged elements
56.	INVECTIVE	Insults
57.	IRKED	Irritated; annoyed
58.	LUDICROUS	Laughable because it's ridiculous or foolish
59.	LURID	Causing shock or horror
60.	MOCK	Imitation; false
61.	MUTINOUS	Rebellious
62.	MUTUAL	Possessed in common
63.	OBTAIN	Get; acquire
64.	OMINOUSLY	Threateningly
65.	OPTIMIST	One who always expects a favorable outcome
66.	PERIL	Danger
67.	PERPETUAL	Lasting forever
68.	PHILANTHROPY	Giving charitable donations or aid
69.	PRECISELY	Exactly
70.	PRECLUDED	Prevented; made impossible by previous action
71.	PRELUDE	Event or action preceding a more important one
72.	PRODIGY	Person with exceptional talents
73.	PROXY	Person authorized to act for another
74.	QUALMS	Issues causing uneasiness
75.	REGIMENTATION	Uniformity and discipline
76.	RENDEZVOUS	Prearranged meeting
77.	REPENTANT	Feeling sorry for a wrong-doing
78.	REPRIMAND	A scolding, punishment or correction for doing something wrong
79.	REPROBATES	Morally unprincipled people
80.	RHETORICAL	Only one or no answer is expected
81.	RIDICULE	Make fun of
82.	SIMULTANEOUS	At the same time
83.	SUBSEQUENT	Following in order
84.	SUBTLE	Not immediately obvious
85.	SULLEN	Showing ill-humor or resentment
86.	SUPPLICATION	Prayer; humble begging
87.	SURGEONS	Doctors who perform operations
88.	SURREPTITIOUS	Performed or acquired by secret means
89.	TACITLY	Without speaking
90.	TOLERATE	Allow without opposing
91.	ULTIMATE	Final; best or most extreme example of its kind
92.	UNANIMOUSLY	In complete agreement
93.	UNREQUITED	Not returned
94.	VERACITY	Truthfulness
95.	VERGED	Came to the edge of
96.	VICINITY	Neighborhood; area
97.	VITALITY	Energy

Cheaper By The Dozen Vocabulary Fill In The Blank 1

_____ 1. Ill; sick

_____ 2. Only one or no answer is expected

_____ 3. Imitation; false

_____ 4. Allow without opposing

_____ 5. A situation requiring a choice

_____ 6. Dislike intensely

_____ 7. An assumed name

_____ 8. Things (usually negative) implied or suggested

_____ 9. Make fun of

_____ 10. One who always expects a favorable outcome

_____ 11. Young woman who is formally presented to society

_____ 12. Terrible; disastrous

_____ 13. Yielded; gave in

_____ 14. Find out

_____ 15. Without speaking

_____ 16. Many complexly arranged elements

_____ 17. Ability

_____ 18. Causing shock or horror

_____ 19. Lazy

_____ 20. Strong belief

Cheaper By The Dozen Vocabulary Fill In The Blank 1 Answer Key

AILING	1. Ill; sick
RHETORICAL	2. Only one or no answer is expected
MOCK	3. Imitation; false
TOLERATE	4. Allow without opposing
DILEMMA	5. A situation requiring a choice
DETEST	6. Dislike intensely
ALIAS	7. An assumed name
INNUENDOES	8. Things (usually negative) implied or suggested
RIDICULE	9. Make fun of
OPTIMIST	10. One who always expects a favorable outcome
DEBUTANTE	11. Young woman who is formally presented to society
DIRE	12. Terrible; disastrous
CAPITULATED	13. Yielded; gave in
ASCERTAIN	14. Find out
TACITLY	15. Without speaking
INTRICACIES	16. Many complexly arranged elements
APTITUDE	17. Ability
LURID	18. Causing shock or horror
INDOLENT	19. Lazy
CONVICTION	20. Strong belief

Cheaper By The Dozen Vocabulary Fill In The Blank 2

_____ 1. Following in order

_____ 2. Home for nuns

_____ 3. One who always expects a favorable outcome

_____ 4. Suggested without directly saying

_____ 5. Things (usually negative) implied or suggested

_____ 6. Feeling sorry for a wrong-doing

_____ 7. Final; best or most extreme example of its kind

_____ 8. Bestowed or given as an honor

_____ 9. Prearranged meeting

_____ 10. Prayer; humble begging

_____ 11. To come between; interfere

_____ 12. Angrily because of something unjust

_____ 13. Find out

_____ 14. Begged for urgently

_____ 15. Many complexly arranged elements

_____ 16. To happen at the same time

_____ 17. Dislike intensely

_____ 18. Morally unprincipled people

_____ 19. List of things to be done

_____ 20. Insults

Cheaper By The Dozen Vocabulary Fill In The Blank 2 Answer Key

SUBSEQUENT	1.	Following in order
CONVENT	2.	Home for nuns
OPTIMIST	3.	One who always expects a favorable outcome
IMPLIED	4.	Suggested without directly saying
INNUENDOES	5.	Things (usually negative) implied or suggested
REPENTANT	6.	Feeling sorry for a wrong-doing
ULTIMATE	7.	Final; best or most extreme example of its kind
CONFERRED	8.	Bestowed or given as an honor
RENDEZVOUS	9.	Prearranged meeting
SUPPLICATION	10.	Prayer; humble begging
INTERVENE	11.	To come between; interfere
INDIGNANTLY	12.	Angrily because of something unjust
ASCERTAIN	13.	Find out
IMPLORED	14.	Begged for urgently
INTRICACIES	15.	Many complexly arranged elements
COINCIDE	16.	To happen at the same time
DETEST	17.	Dislike intensely
REPROBATES	18.	Morally unprincipled people
AGENDA	19.	List of things to be done
INVECTIVE	20.	Insults

Cheaper By The Dozen Vocabulary Fill In The Blank 3

_____ 1. Exceptionally bad

_____ 2. Settled securely

_____ 3. Laughable because it's ridiculous or foolish

_____ 4. Truthfulness

_____ 5. Young woman who is formally presented to society

_____ 6. To come forth from; come into sight

_____ 7. Prevented; made impossible by previous action

_____ 8. Final; best or most extreme example of its kind

_____ 9. Give up

_____ 10. Enjoyable; delightful

_____ 11. Not returned

_____ 12. Danger

_____ 13. Bestowed or given as an honor

_____ 14. A reward offered to motivate one to action

_____ 15. Showing ill-humor or resentment

_____ 16. Not immediately obvious

_____ 17. Harmless

_____ 18. Dislike intensely

_____ 19. Find out

_____ 20. Ill; sick

Cheaper By The Dozen Vocabulary Fill In The Blank 3 Answer Key

ATROCIOUS	1. Exceptionally bad
ENSCONCED	2. Settled securely
LUDICROUS	3. Laughable because it's ridiculous or foolish
VERACITY	4. Truthfulness
DEBUTANTE	5. Young woman who is formally presented to society
EMERGE	6. To come forth from; come into sight
PRECLUDED	7. Prevented; made impossible by previous action
ULTIMATE	8. Final; best or most extreme example of its kind
FORGO	9. Give up
DELECTABLE	10. Enjoyable; delightful
UNREQUITED	11. Not returned
PERIL	12. Danger
CONFERRED	13. Bestowed or given as an honor
INCENTIVE	14. A reward offered to motivate one to action
SULLEN	15. Showing ill-humor or resentment
SUBTLE	16. Not immediately obvious
INNOCUOUS	17. Harmless
DETEST	18. Dislike intensely
ASCERTAIN	19. Find out
AILING	20. Ill; sick

Cheaper By The Dozen Vocabulary Fill In The Blank 4

1. Self-assertiveness
2. Unavoidable; going to happen no matter what
3. Harmless
4. Began
5. To follow immediately after
6. An emotion of respect and wonder tinged with fear
7. Exceptionally bad
8. Savage fierceness
9. At the same time
10. Person with exceptional talents
11. To have a necessary accompaniment or consequences
12. Giving charitable donations or aid
13. Energy
14. Rebellious
15. Release from entanglement
16. A situation requiring a choice
17. Strong belief
18. Find out
19. Grateful
20. Ill; sick

Cheaper By The Dozen Vocabulary Fill In The Blank 4 Answer Key

GALL	1. Self-assertiveness
INEVITABLE	2. Unavoidable; going to happen no matter what
INNOCUOUS	3. Harmless
INAUGURATED	4. Began
ENSUE	5. To follow immediately after
AWE	6. An emotion of respect and wonder tinged with fear
ATROCIOUS	7. Exceptionally bad
FEROCITY	8. Savage fierceness
SIMULTANEOUS	9. At the same time
PRODIGY	10. Person with exceptional talents
ENTAIL	11. To have a necessary accompaniment or consequences
PHILANTHROPY	12. Giving charitable donations or aid
VITALITY	13. Energy
MUTINOUS	14. Rebellious
EXTRICATE	15. Release from entanglement
DILEMMA	16. A situation requiring a choice
CONVICTION	17. Strong belief
ASCERTAIN	18. Find out
APPRECIATIVE	19. Grateful
AILING	20. Ill; sick

Cheaper By The Dozen Vocabulary Matching 1

___ 1. SIMULTANEOUS   A. To follow immediately after
___ 2. INEVITABLE   B. Begged for urgently
___ 3. PROXY   C. Ill; sick
___ 4. EXTRICATE   D. Terrible; disastrous
___ 5. AWE   E. Threateningly
___ 6. ATROCIOUS   F. Exceptionally bad
___ 7. OBTAIN   G. An emotion of respect and wonder tinged with fear
___ 8. SUPPLICATION   H. Prayer; humble begging
___ 9. DETEST   I. Not returned
___10. SUBTLE   J. Social outcasts
___11. EMERGE   K. Get; acquire
___12. INNOCUOUS   L. Uniformity and discipline
___13. ASCERTAIN   M. Home for nuns
___14. UNREQUITED   N. Dislike intensely
___15. INVECTIVE   O. Person authorized to act for another
___16. AILING   P. Find out
___17. DERELICTS   Q. Unavoidable; going to happen no matter what
___18. OMINOUSLY   R. To come forth from; come into sight
___19. SUBSEQUENT   S. Insults
___20. IMPLORED   T. At the same time
___21. ULTIMATE   U. Final; best or most extreme example of its kind
___22. DIRE   V. Not immediately obvious
___23. ENSUE   W. Harmless
___24. REGIMENTATION   X. Following in order
___25. CONVENT   Y. Release from entanglement

Cheaper By The Dozen Vocabulary Matching 1 Answer Key

T - 1. SIMULTANEOUS		A. To follow immediately after
Q - 2. INEVITABLE		B. Begged for urgently
O - 3. PROXY		C. Ill; sick
Y - 4. EXTRICATE		D. Terrible; disastrous
G - 5. AWE		E. Threateningly
F - 6. ATROCIOUS		F. Exceptionally bad
K - 7. OBTAIN		G. An emotion of respect and wonder tinged with fear
H - 8. SUPPLICATION		H. Prayer; humble begging
N - 9. DETEST		I. Not returned
V - 10. SUBTLE		J. Social outcasts
R - 11. EMERGE		K. Get; acquire
W - 12. INNOCUOUS		L. Uniformity and discipline
P - 13. ASCERTAIN		M. Home for nuns
I - 14. UNREQUITED		N. Dislike intensely
S - 15. INVECTIVE		O. Person authorized to act for another
C - 16. AILING		P. Find out
J - 17. DERELICTS		Q. Unavoidable; going to happen no matter what
E - 18. OMINOUSLY		R. To come forth from; come into sight
X - 19. SUBSEQUENT		S. Insults
B - 20. IMPLORED		T. At the same time
U - 21. ULTIMATE		U. Final; best or most extreme example of its kind
D - 22. DIRE		V. Not immediately obvious
A - 23. ENSUE		W. Harmless
L - 24. REGIMENTATION		X. Following in order
M - 25. CONVENT		Y. Release from entanglement

Cheaper By The Dozen Vocabulary Matching 2

___ 1. CALLIOPE   A. Musical keyboard fitted with steam whistles
___ 2. FEROCITY   B. Strong belief
___ 3. INCENTIVE   C. Prayer; humble begging
___ 4. AGENDA   D. Person with exceptional talents
___ 5. REPROBATES   E. Home for nuns
___ 6. DORY   F. Accompanied by or filled with something undesirable
___ 7. CONVENT   G. Imitation; false
___ 8. REGIMENTATION   H. An emotion of respect and wonder tinged with fear
___ 9. RHETORICAL   I. Savage fierceness
___ 10. FRAUGHT   J. Noisy uproar and confusion
___ 11. INEVITABLE   K. Small, narrow, flat-bottomed boat
___ 12. OBTAIN   L. At the same time
___ 13. SIMULTANEOUS   M. Performed or acquired by secret means
___ 14. SULLEN   N. Showing ill-humor or resentment
___ 15. PRODIGY   O. Lazy
___ 16. AWE   P. Morally unprincipled people
___ 17. SUPPLICATION   Q. Unavoidable; going to happen no matter what
___ 18. BEDLAM   R. Uniformity and discipline
___ 19. INDOLENT   S. A reward offered to motivate one to action
___ 20. CONVICTION   T. Get; acquire
___ 21. MOCK   U. List of things to be done
___ 22. PRELUDE   V. A situation requiring a choice
___ 23. ASCERTAIN   W. Event or action preceding a more important one
___ 24. SURREPTITIOUS   X. Only one or no answer is expected
___ 25. DILEMMA   Y. Find out

Cheaper By The Dozen Vocabulary Matching 2 Answer Key

A - 1.	CALLIOPE	A. Musical keyboard fitted with steam whistles
I - 2.	FEROCITY	B. Strong belief
S - 3.	INCENTIVE	C. Prayer; humble begging
U - 4.	AGENDA	D. Person with exceptional talents
P - 5.	REPROBATES	E. Home for nuns
K - 6.	DORY	F. Accompanied by or filled with something undesirable
E - 7.	CONVENT	G. Imitation; false
R - 8.	REGIMENTATION	H. An emotion of respect and wonder tinged with fear
X - 9.	RHETORICAL	I. Savage fierceness
F - 10.	FRAUGHT	J. Noisy uproar and confusion
Q - 11.	INEVITABLE	K. Small, narrow, flat-bottomed boat
T - 12.	OBTAIN	L. At the same time
L - 13.	SIMULTANEOUS	M. Performed or acquired by secret means
N - 14.	SULLEN	N. Showing ill-humor or resentment
D - 15.	PRODIGY	O. Lazy
H - 16.	AWE	P. Morally unprincipled people
C - 17.	SUPPLICATION	Q. Unavoidable; going to happen no matter what
J - 18.	BEDLAM	R. Uniformity and discipline
O - 19.	INDOLENT	S. A reward offered to motivate one to action
B - 20.	CONVICTION	T. Get; acquire
G - 21.	MOCK	U. List of things to be done
W - 22.	PRELUDE	V. A situation requiring a choice
Y - 23.	ASCERTAIN	W. Event or action preceding a more important one
M - 24.	SURREPTITIOUS	X. Only one or no answer is expected
V - 25.	DILEMMA	Y. Find out

Cheaper By The Dozen Vocabulary Matching 3

___ 1. MOCK   A. Disaster
___ 2. ENSCONCED   B. Strong belief
___ 3. IMPLORED   C. Final; best or most extreme example of its kind
___ 4. ATROCIOUS   D. Imitation; false
___ 5. OBTAIN   E. Person authorized to act for another
___ 6. ADMONISHED   F. Angrily because of something unjust
___ 7. PRECISELY   G. Lazy
___ 8. CONCEDED   H. Kindly but seriously reprimanded
___ 9. CONTAGIOUS   I. Get; acquire
___ 10. CONVICTION   J. An emotion of respect and wonder tinged with fear
___ 11. INDIGNANTLY   K. Admitted; acknowledged as true
___ 12. INDOLENT   L. One who always expects a favorable outcome
___ 13. IMPLIED   M. Exceptionally bad
___ 14. INVECTIVE   N. At the same time
___ 15. OPTIMIST   O. Insults
___ 16. SURGEONS   P. Settled securely
___ 17. INTRICACIES   Q. Accompanied by or filled with something undesirable
___ 18. PROXY   R. Musical keyboard fitted with steam whistles
___ 19. DEBACLE   S. Uniformity and discipline
___ 20. REGIMENTATION   T. Begged for urgently
___ 21. CALLIOPE   U. Exactly
___ 22. AWE   V. Doctors who perform operations
___ 23. FRAUGHT   W. Tending to spread from one to another
___ 24. ULTIMATE   X. Suggested without directly saying
___ 25. SIMULTANEOUS   Y. Many complexly arranged elements

Cheaper By The Dozen Vocabulary Matching 3 Answer Key

D - 1. MOCK   A. Disaster
P - 2. ENSCONCED   B. Strong belief
T - 3. IMPLORED   C. Final; best or most extreme example of its kind
M - 4. ATROCIOUS   D. Imitation; false
I - 5. OBTAIN   E. Person authorized to act for another
H - 6. ADMONISHED   F. Angrily because of something unjust
U - 7. PRECISELY   G. Lazy
K - 8. CONCEDED   H. Kindly but seriously reprimanded
W - 9. CONTAGIOUS   I. Get; acquire
B - 10. CONVICTION   J. An emotion of respect and wonder tinged with fear
F - 11. INDIGNANTLY   K. Admitted; acknowledged as true
G - 12. INDOLENT   L. One who always expects a favorable outcome
X - 13. IMPLIED   M. Exceptionally bad
O - 14. INVECTIVE   N. At the same time
L - 15. OPTIMIST   O. Insults
V - 16. SURGEONS   P. Settled securely
Y - 17. INTRICACIES   Q. Accompanied by or filled with something undesirable
E - 18. PROXY   R. Musical keyboard fitted with steam whistles
A - 19. DEBACLE   S. Uniformity and discipline
S - 20. REGIMENTATION T. Begged for urgently
R - 21. CALLIOPE   U. Exactly
J - 22. AWE   V. Doctors who perform operations
Q - 23. FRAUGHT   W. Tending to spread from one to another
C - 24. ULTIMATE   X. Suggested without directly saying
N - 25. SIMULTANEOUS Y. Many complexly arranged elements

Cheaper By The Dozen Vocabulary Matching 4

___ 1. CONCEDED   A. Small, narrow, flat-bottomed boat
___ 2. ULTIMATE   B. Truthfulness
___ 3. SURGEONS   C. Tending to spread from one to another
___ 4. CONTAGIOUS   D. Noisy uproar and confusion
___ 5. INEVITABLE   E. Young woman who is formally presented to society
___ 6. UNREQUITED   F. Many complexly arranged elements
___ 7. MUTINOUS   G. Unavoidable; going to happen no matter what
___ 8. RIDICULE   H. Imitation; false
___ 9. CONVENT   I. To follow immediately after
___10. DEBUTANTE   J. Energy
___11. MOCK   K. To come between; interfere
___12. PRELUDE   L. Not returned
___13. IMPLIED   M. Home for nuns
___14. INNUENDOES   N. Suggested without directly saying
___15. DORY   O. Things (usually negative) implied or suggested
___16. INTERVENE   P. Lazy
___17. VERACITY   Q. Make fun of
___18. BENEVOLENT   R. Doctors who perform operations
___19. REPRIMAND   S. Enjoyable; delightful
___20. INTRICACIES   T. Event or action preceding a more important one
___21. VITALITY   U. Kind; charitable
___22. ENSUE   V. A scolding, punishment or correction for doing something wrong
___23. INDOLENT   W. Admitted; acknowledged as true
___24. DELECTABLE   X. Final; best or most extreme example of its kind
___25. BEDLAM   Y. Rebellious

Cheaper By The Dozen Vocabulary Matching 4 Answer Key

W - 1.	CONCEDED	A. Small, narrow, flat-bottomed boat
X - 2.	ULTIMATE	B. Truthfulness
R - 3.	SURGEONS	C. Tending to spread from one to another
C - 4.	CONTAGIOUS	D. Noisy uproar and confusion
G - 5.	INEVITABLE	E. Young woman who is formally presented to society
L - 6.	UNREQUITED	F. Many complexly arranged elements
Y - 7.	MUTINOUS	G. Unavoidable; going to happen no matter what
Q - 8.	RIDICULE	H. Imitation; false
M - 9.	CONVENT	I. To follow immediately after
E - 10.	DEBUTANTE	J. Energy
H - 11.	MOCK	K. To come between; interfere
T - 12.	PRELUDE	L. Not returned
N - 13.	IMPLIED	M. Home for nuns
O - 14.	INNUENDOES	N. Suggested without directly saying
A - 15.	DORY	O. Things (usually negative) implied or suggested
K - 16.	INTERVENE	P. Lazy
B - 17.	VERACITY	Q. Make fun of
U - 18.	BENEVOLENT	R. Doctors who perform operations
V - 19.	REPRIMAND	S. Enjoyable; delightful
F - 20.	INTRICACIES	T. Event or action preceding a more important one
J - 21.	VITALITY	U. Kind; charitable
I - 22.	ENSUE	V. A scolding, punishment or correction for doing something wrong
P - 23.	INDOLENT	W. Admitted; acknowledged as true
S - 24.	DELECTABLE	X. Final; best or most extreme example of its kind
D - 25.	BEDLAM	Y. Rebellious

Cheaper By The Dozen Vocabulary Magic Squares 1

Match the definition with the vocabulary word. Put your answers in the magic squares below. When your answers are correct, all columns and rows will add to the same number.

A. EXTRICATE	E. CONCEDED	I. ALIAS	M. DEBACLE
B. MUTUAL	F. BELLIGERENT	J. PRECISELY	N. SULLEN
C. INNOCUOUS	G. ULTIMATE	K. CONFERRED	O. ENSUE
D. OPTIMIST	H. BENEVOLENT	L. SIMULTANEOUS	P. LURID

1. To follow immediately after
2. Exactly
3. Kind; charitable
4. Release from entanglement
5. One who always expects a favorable outcome
6. Admitted; acknowledged as true
7. Bestowed or given as an honor
8. Showing ill-humor or resentment
9. Aggressive; hostile
10. Harmless
11. Disaster
12. At the same time
13. An assumed name
14. Causing shock or horror
15. Possessed in common
16. Final; best or most extreme example of its kind

A=	B=	C=	D=
E=	F=	G=	H=
I=	J=	K=	L=
M=	N=	O=	P=

Cheaper By The Dozen Vocabulary Magic Squares 1 Answer Key

Match the definition with the vocabulary word. Put your answers in the magic squares below. When your answers are correct, all columns and rows will add to the same number.

A. EXTRICATE
B. MUTUAL
C. INNOCUOUS
D. OPTIMIST
E. CONCEDED
F. BELLIGERENT
G. ULTIMATE
H. BENEVOLENT
I. ALIAS
J. PRECISELY
K. CONFERRED
L. SIMULTANEOUS
M. DEBACLE
N. SULLEN
O. ENSUE
P. LURID

1. To follow immediately after
2. Exactly
3. Kind; charitable
4. Release from entanglement
5. One who always expects a favorable outcome
6. Admitted; acknowledged as true
7. Bestowed or given as an honor
8. Showing ill-humor or resentment
9. Aggressive; hostile
10. Harmless
11. Disaster
12. At the same time
13. An assumed name
14. Causing shock or horror
15. Possessed in common
16. Final; best or most extreme example of its kind

A=4	B=15	C=10	D=5
E=6	F=9	G=16	H=3
I=13	J=2	K=7	L=12
M=11	N=8	O=1	P=14

Cheaper By The Dozen Vocabulary Magic Squares 2

Match the definition with the vocabulary word. Put your answers in the magic squares below. When your answers are correct, all columns and rows will add to the same number.

A. PERPETUAL   E. DERELICTS   I. FORGO   M. PERIL
B. PRECLUDED   F. MOCK   J. SURREPTITIOUS   N. CONVICTION
C. SUPPLICATION   G. GALL   K. INVECTIVE   O. CONTAGIOUS
D. VERACITY   H. VERGED   L. INCENTIVE   P. INEVITABLE

1. Came to the edge of
2. Danger
3. Prevented; made impossible by previous action
4. Insults
5. Performed or acquired by secret means
6. Prayer; humble begging
7. Unavoidable; going to happen no matter what
8. Social outcasts
9. Tending to spread from one to another
10. Imitation; false
11. Give up
12. Truthfulness
13. Lasting forever
14. A reward offered to motivate one to action
15. Self-assertiveness
16. Strong belief

A=	B=	C=	D=
E=	F=	G=	H=
I=	J=	K=	L=
M=	N=	O=	P=

Cheaper By The Dozen Vocabulary Magic Squares 2 Answer Key

Match the definition with the vocabulary word. Put your answers in the magic squares below. When your answers are correct, all columns and rows will add to the same number.

A. PERPETUAL
B. PRECLUDED
C. SUPPLICATION
D. VERACITY
E. DERELICTS
F. MOCK
G. GALL
H. VERGED
I. FORGO
J. SURREPTITIOUS
K. INVECTIVE
L. INCENTIVE
M. PERIL
N. CONVICTION
O. CONTAGIOUS
P. INEVITABLE

1. Came to the edge of
2. Danger
3. Prevented; made impossible by previous action
4. Insults
5. Performed or acquired by secret means
6. Prayer; humble begging
7. Unavoidable; going to happen no matter what
8. Social outcasts
9. Tending to spread from one to another
10. Imitation; false
11. Give up
12. Truthfulness
13. Lasting forever
14. A reward offered to motivate one to action
15. Self-assertiveness
16. Strong belief

A=13	B=3	C=6	D=12
E=8	F=10	G=15	H=1
I=11	J=5	K=4	L=14
M=2	N=16	O=9	P=7

Cheaper By The Dozen Vocabulary Magic Squares 3

Match the definition with the vocabulary word. Put your answers in the magic squares below. When your answers are correct, all columns and rows will add to the same number.

A. DOCILE	E. OMINOUSLY	I. EMERGE	M. CONCEDED
B. QUALMS	F. AGENDA	J. BENEVOLENT	N. MOCK
C. VERGED	G. PRODIGY	K. DETEST	O. REPENTANT
D. UNREQUITED	H. RIDICULE	L. EXTRICATE	P. TACITLY

1. Make fun of
2. Obedient; submissive to management
3. Issues causing uneasiness
4. Person with exceptional talents
5. Kind; charitable
6. Feeling sorry for a wrong-doing
7. Without speaking
8. To come forth from; come into sight
9. Dislike intensely
10. Imitation; false
11. Admitted; acknowledged as true
12. Release from entanglement
13. Threateningly
14. Not returned
15. Came to the edge of
16. List of things to be done

A=	B=	C=	D=
E=	F=	G=	H=
I=	J=	K=	L=
M=	N=	O=	P=

Cheaper By The Dozen Vocabulary Magic Squares 3 Answer Key

Match the definition with the vocabulary word. Put your answers in the magic squares below. When your answers are correct, all columns and rows will add to the same number.

A. DOCILE
B. QUALMS
C. VERGED
D. UNREQUITED
E. OMINOUSLY
F. AGENDA
G. PRODIGY
H. RIDICULE
I. EMERGE
J. BENEVOLENT
K. DETEST
L. EXTRICATE
M. CONCEDED
N. MOCK
O. REPENTANT
P. TACITLY

1. Make fun of
2. Obedient; submissive to management
3. Issues causing uneasiness
4. Person with exceptional talents
5. Kind; charitable
6. Feeling sorry for a wrong-doing
7. Without speaking
8. To come forth from; come into sight
9. Dislike intensely
10. Imitation; false
11. Admitted; acknowledged as true
12. Release from entanglement
13. Threateningly
14. Not returned
15. Came to the edge of
16. List of things to be done

A=2	B=3	C=15	D=14
E=13	F=16	G=4	H=1
I=8	J=5	K=9	L=12
M=11	N=10	O=6	P=7

Cheaper By The Dozen Vocabulary Magic Squares 4

Match the definition with the vocabulary word. Put your answers in the magic squares below. When your answers are correct, all columns and rows will add to the same number.

A. CONTAGIOUS
B. CAUCUS
C. APPRECIATIVE
D. CONFERRED
E. PRECLUDED
F. ATROCIOUS
G. INDICATE
H. IMPLIED
I. OPTIMIST
J. DIRE
K. LUDICROUS
L. MUTUAL
M. MOCK
N. VITALITY
O. INCENTIVE
P. INVECTIVE

1. A reward offered to motivate one to action
2. Bestowed or given as an honor
3. Terrible; disastrous
4. Prevented; made impossible by previous action
5. One who always expects a favorable outcome
6. Exceptionally bad
7. Insults
8. Grateful
9. Suggested without directly saying
10. Laughable because it's ridiculous or foolish
11. Tending to spread from one to another
12. Energy
13. A meeting to decide upon questions of policy
14. Imitation; false
15. Demonstrate or point out
16. Possessed in common

A=	B=	C=	D=
E=	F=	G=	H=
I=	J=	K=	L=
M=	N=	O=	P=

Cheaper By The Dozen Vocabulary Magic Squares 4 Answer Key

Match the definition with the vocabulary word. Put your answers in the magic squares below. When your answers are correct, all columns and rows will add to the same number.

A. CONTAGIOUS
B. CAUCUS
C. APPRECIATIVE
D. CONFERRED
E. PRECLUDED
F. ATROCIOUS
G. INDICATE
H. IMPLIED
I. OPTIMIST
J. DIRE
K. LUDICROUS
L. MUTUAL
M. MOCK
N. VITALITY
O. INCENTIVE
P. INVECTIVE

1. A reward offered to motivate one to action
2. Bestowed or given as an honor
3. Terrible; disastrous
4. Prevented; made impossible by previous action
5. One who always expects a favorable outcome
6. Exceptionally bad
7. Insults
8. Grateful
9. Suggested without directly saying
10. Laughable because it's ridiculous or foolish
11. Tending to spread from one to another
12. Energy
13. A meeting to decide upon questions of policy
14. Imitation; false
15. Demonstrate or point out
16. Possessed in common

A=11	B=13	C=8	D=2
E=4	F=6	G=15	H=9
I=5	J=3	K=10	L=16
M=14	N=12	O=1	P=7

Cheaper By The Dozen Vocabulary Word Search 1

```
D O P T I M I S T N E L O V E N E B
N O D A N C M F N R M A I K Y H I T
O N C C D O P O E W E U R W V S N K
I I M I O N L R V D R T K Y L T C X
T A U T L C O G N I G U E M S C R S
A T T L E E R O O L E M D U F I E S
C R I Y N D E R C E P R O X Y L D F
I E N Y T E D H N M H E P P H E U V
L C O M C D P Z C M N R X J V R L N
P S U O I C O R T A E B Y A W E O Q
P A S M O C K W T C U L W P N D U Q
U W M H P Q Y L I Z S C S S B S S E
S N O E G R U S S U R V U G A L L J
D M R R M M E A O P Z E B S G C Y V
Z I R T I L I M L Q L R T L A N S G
L F R S Y L I D I M X G L B E D N M
K Y M E A N J O A P S E E L I I K V
S E I C A C I R T N I D L R L D W S
F K C N W W S Y N F Q U U I C S D C
E L U C I D I R E B S L A G E N D A
```

A meeting to decide upon questions of policy (6)
A situation requiring a choice (7)
Admitted; acknowledged as true (8)
An assumed name (5)
An emotion of respect and wonder tinged with fear (3)
At the same time (12)
Begged for urgently (8)
Came to the edge of (6)
Causing shock or horror (5)
Danger (5)
Disaster (7)
Doctors who perform operations (8)
Exactly (9)
Exceptionally bad (9)
Expressing disbelief (13)
Find out (9)
Give up (5)
Home for nuns (7)
Ill; sick (6)
Imitation; false (4)
In complete agreement (11)
Irritated; annoyed (5)
Issues causing uneasiness (6)
Kind; charitable (10)
Lazy (8)
List of things to be done (6)
Make fun of (8)
Many complexly arranged elements (11)
Not immediately obvious (6)
Obedient; submissive to management (6)
One who always expects a favorable outcome (8)
Person authorized to act for another (5)
Possessed in common (6)
Prayer; humble begging (12)
Rebellious (8)
Self-assertiveness (4)
Showing ill-humor or resentment (6)
Small, narrow, flat-bottomed boat (4)
Social outcasts (9)
Terrible; disastrous (4)
To come forth from; come into sight (6)
To follow immediately after (5)
To have a necessary accompaniment or consequences (6)
Without speaking (7)

Cheaper By The Dozen Vocabulary Word Search 1 Answer Key

```
D  O  P  T  I  M  I  S  T  N  E  L  O  V  E  N  E  B
N  O     A  N  C  M  F  N     M  A     I        I
O  N  C  C  D  O  P  O  E     E  U  R        S  N
I  I  M  I  O  N  L  R  V  D  R  K           T  C
T  A  U  T  L  C  O  G  N  I  G  U  E     S  C  R
A  T  T  L  E  E  R  O  O  L  E  M  D  U     I  E
C  R  I  Y  N  D  E  C  E  P  R  O  X  Y     L  D
I  E  N     T  E  D     M     E  P           E  U
L  C  O        D        C  M  N              R  L
P  S  U  O  I  C  O  R  T  A  E     Y  A  W  E  O
P  A  S  M  O  C  K     T  C  U  L     N  D     U
U        P  Q     L  I     S  C  S  S        S  E
S  N  O  E  G  R  U  S  S  U     V  U  G  A  L  L
D     R     M  E  A  O        E  B  S     C  Y
         I        L  I  M     R  T     A  N     G
   L  R  S  Y  L  I  D  I  M  G  L  B  E  D  N
         E  A  N     O  A     S  E  E  L  I  I
S  E  I  C  A  C  I  R  T  N  I  D  L  R  L
            N        Y  N           U  U  I
E  L  U  C  I  D  I  R  E     S  L  A  G  E  N  D  A
```

A meeting to decide upon questions of policy (6)
A situation requiring a choice (7)
Admitted; acknowledged as true (8)
An assumed name (5)
An emotion of respect and wonder tinged with fear (3)
At the same time (12)
Begged for urgently (8)
Came to the edge of (6)
Causing shock or horror (5)
Danger (5)
Disaster (7)
Doctors who perform operations (8)
Exactly (9)
Exceptionally bad (9)
Expressing disbelief (13)
Find out (9)
Give up (5)
Home for nuns (7)
Ill; sick (6)
Imitation; false (4)
In complete agreement (11)
Irritated; annoyed (5)
Issues causing uneasiness (6)
Kind; charitable (10)

Lazy (8)
List of things to be done (6)
Make fun of (8)
Many complexly arranged elements (11)
Not immediately obvious (6)
Obedient; submissive to management (6)
One who always expects a favorable outcome (8)
Person authorized to act for another (5)
Possessed in common (6)
Prayer; humble begging (12)
Rebellious (8)
Self-assertiveness (4)
Showing ill-humor or resentment (6)
Small, narrow, flat-bottomed boat (4)
Social outcasts (9)
Terrible; disastrous (4)
To come forth from; come into sight (6)
To follow immediately after (5)
To have a necessary accompaniment or consequences (6)
Without speaking (7)

Cheaper By The Dozen Vocabulary Word Search 2

```
O S V D P E Y T I C A R E V D M E P C Z
P U E E H R M N R P R Q L E E U N R O J
T L R L I A E E D I E G K L B T S O N X
I L G E L D S L R G D R Y C A I U X V M
M E E C A M S O U G I I M C N E Y E M
I N D T N O V M D E G C L L O L T R P
S J C A T N O E K O E J H U E U T I G J
T Z A B H I I N D I C A T E L S B N E P
H Z U L R S C E T D O K J L G E U I D F
G M C E O H O B O E N G A T L S S C O E
U E U H P E R K L T C G C L A T F I C R
A V S T Y D T L E E E Z I A N C N V I O
R I P J U D A J R S D G O J L I I Y L C
F T Y B Y A I X A T E S B L K L B T E I
E N T A I L L R T R D S T S U E I T L T
R E P R O B A T E S E W A R H R D O R Y
L C X E D I C N I O C I I P C E I V P F
E N E V R E T N I L L H N L F D B D D E
A I L I N G S M L A U Q A P T I T U D E
P Y W P M G Q D S Q S K M N J W N J D Y
```

A meeting to decide upon questions of policy (6)
A reward offered to motivate one to action (9)
Ability (8)
Accompanied by or filled with something undesirable (7)
Admitted; acknowledged as true (8)
Aggressive; hostile (11)
Allow without opposing (8)
An assumed name (5)
An emotion of respect and wonder tinged with fear (3)
Approached the same point from different directions (9)
Came to the edge of (6)
Causing shock or horror (5)
Danger (5)
Demonstrate or point out (8)
Disaster (7)
Dislike intensely (6)
Enjoyable; delightful (10)
Event or action preceding a more important one (7)
Exceptionally bad (9)
Get; acquire (6)
Giving charitable donations or aid (12)
Ill; sick (6)
Imitation; false (4)
Irritated; annoyed (5)

Issues causing uneasiness (6)
Kind; charitable (10)
Kindly but seriously reprimanded (10)
Make fun of (8)
Morally unprincipled people (10)
Musical keyboard fitted with steam whistles (8)
Neighborhood; area (8)
Not immediately obvious (6)
Obedient; submissive to management (6)
One who always expects a favorable outcome (8)
Person authorized to act for another (5)
Possessed in common (6)
Rebellious (8)
Savage fierceness (8)
Self-assertiveness (4)
Showing ill-humor or resentment (6)
Small, narrow, flat-bottomed boat (4)
Social outcasts (9)
Terrible; disastrous (4)
To come between; interfere (9)
To come forth from; come into sight (6)
To follow immediately after (5)
To happen at the same time (8)
To have a necessary accompaniment or consequences (6)
Truthfulness (8)
Without speaking (7)

Cheaper By The Dozen Vocabulary Word Search 2 Answer Key

A meeting to decide upon questions of policy (6)
A reward offered to motivate one to action (9)
Ability (8)
Accompanied by or filled with something undesirable (7)
Admitted; acknowledged as true (8)
Aggressive; hostile (11)
Allow without opposing (8)
An assumed name (5)
An emotion of respect and wonder tinged with fear (3)
Approached the same point from different directions (9)
Came to the edge of (6)
Causing shock or horror (5)
Danger (5)
Demonstrate or point out (8)
Disaster (7)
Dislike intensely (6)
Enjoyable; delightful (10)
Event or action preceding a more important one (7)
Exceptionally bad (9)
Get; acquire (6)
Giving charitable donations or aid (12)
Ill; sick (6)
Imitation; false (4)
Irritated; annoyed (5)

Issues causing uneasiness (6)
Kind; charitable (10)
Kindly but seriously reprimanded (10)
Make fun of (8)
Morally unprincipled people (10)
Musical keyboard fitted with steam whistles (8)
Neighborhood; area (8)
Not immediately obvious (6)
Obedient; submissive to management (6)
One who always expects a favorable outcome (8)
Person authorized to act for another (5)
Possessed in common (6)
Rebellious (8)
Savage fierceness (8)
Self-assertiveness (4)
Showing ill-humor or resentment (6)
Small, narrow, flat-bottomed boat (4)
Social outcasts (9)
Terrible; disastrous (4)
To come between; interfere (9)
To come forth from; come into sight (6)
To follow immediately after (5)
To happen at the same time (8)
To have a necessary accompaniment or consequences (6)
Truthfulness (8)
Without speaking (7)

Cheaper By The Dozen Vocabulary Word Search 3

```
I  N  N  O  C  U  O  U  S  W  L  K  M  V  E  R  G  E  D  J
O  R  E  N  D  E  Z  V  O  U  S  U  M  U  L  Y  F  T  U  Z
M  B  D  C  G  M  S  B  T  B  D  L  V  V  T  T  T  X  N  X
I  M  T  Y  O  U  M  E  N  V  V  T  Z  F  B  I  H  X  R  W
N  N  E  A  C  N  P  D  E  E  G  I  C  L  U  N  N  D  E  K
O  T  T  U  I  Y  T  L  R  P  C  M  L  C  S  I  O  O  Q  M
U  R  A  G  E  N  D  A  E  E  W  A  T  R  O  C  I  O  U  S
S  C  R  C  E  O  C  M  G  R  G  T  L  M  I  I  F  T  I  S
L  X  E  L  I  I  D  W  I  I  J  E  P  L  N  V  U  D  T  P
Y  H  L  V  T  T  I  B  L  L  O  B  E  E  I  A  R  O  E  X
V  U  O  Y  E  C  L  S  L  A  T  U  T  T  L  O  E  R  D  X
S  S  T  T  N  I  E  Y  E  P  S  A  S  A  G  P  P  Y  E  S
I  Q  L  I  T  V  M  F  B  T  C  S  L  C  D  R  R  E  D  X
N  M  U  L  A  N  M  B  P  I  A  I  L  I  N  G  I  N  E  Z
D  O  R  A  I  O  A  R  R  T  D  D  R  D  A  K  M  S  C  S
O  C  I  T  L  C  Z  T  E  U  K  E  F  N  Z  S  A  U  N  X
L  K  D  I  D  M  X  R  L  D  P  T  T  I  K  F  N  E  O  D
E  H  K  V  D  E  S  D  U  E  E  G  R  E  M  E  D  P  C  N
N  F  O  R  G  O  R  I  D  I  C  U  L  E  S  P  R  O  X  Y
T  I  R  K  E  D  P  F  E  R  O  C  I  T  Y  T  T  F  W  B
```

AGENDA	CONTAGIOUS	FEROCITY	OBTAIN	TACITLY
AILING	CONVICTION	FORGO	OMINOUSLY	TOLERATE
ALIAS	DETEST	GALL	PERIL	ULTIMATE
APTITUDE	DILEMMA	INDICATE	PRELUDE	UNREQUITED
ATROCIOUS	DIRE	INDOLENT	PROXY	VERACITY
AWE	DOCILE	INNOCUOUS	QUALMS	VERGED
BEDLAM	DORY	IRKED	RENDEZVOUS	VICINITY
BELLIGERENT	EMERGE	LURID	REPRIMAND	VITALITY
CALLIOPE	ENSUE	MOCK	RIDICULE	
CAUCUS	ENTAIL	MUTINOUS	SUBTLE	
CONCEDED	EXTRICATE	MUTUAL	SULLEN	

Cheaper By The Dozen Vocabulary Word Search 3 Answer Key

[word search grid]

AGENDA	CONTAGIOUS	FEROCITY	OBTAIN	TACITLY
AILING	CONVICTION	FORGO	OMINOUSLY	TOLERATE
ALIAS	DETEST	GALL	PERIL	ULTIMATE
APTITUDE	DILEMMA	INDICATE	PRELUDE	UNREQUITED
ATROCIOUS	DIRE	INDOLENT	PROXY	VERACITY
AWE	DOCILE	INNOCUOUS	QUALMS	VERGED
BEDLAM	DORY	IRKED	RENDEZVOUS	VICINITY
BELLIGERENT	EMERGE	LURID	REPRIMAND	VITALITY
CALLIOPE	ENSUE	MOCK	RIDICULE	
CAUCUS	ENTAIL	MUTINOUS	SUBTLE	
CONCEDED	EXTRICATE	MUTUAL	SULLEN	

Cheaper By The Dozen Vocabulary Word Search 4

```
D E D E C N O C S N E T A L I A S I G G
E O B G N I L I A U S H S U L L E N A H
B E C N P Q P L M I B T L D E B A C L E
U M R I D R P Y M P C S M L A U Q E L X
T E E A L S O I E I L V E D Y I D N J S
A R G T K E T D L C S I N Q N T C T S Y
N G I R P P W E I R O E E T U N D I U L
T E M E O D R T D G G B E D D E E V R X
E K E C K E S B M A Y R T E T L N E G K
M T N S D I V H C U V P R A T O G T E Y
F L T A L T P Y D E T O R B I D L L O Y
F A A A T Z E O N F L U U O E N J I N Z
V Y T I C O R E F P G S A Y X I P A S S
X A I I P Y I S M U C W F L T Y P T D H
F W O L G D L I A V G L M F R T S N I W
R P N M H U D N T C D B R O I U N E R D
E N S U E V I T C E V N I T C I R K E D
B E D L A M R N J B W V U U A K S P N G
V E R G E D U G G G K D A S T F O R G O
R I D I C U L E W A E C T S E T E D C R
```

AGENDA	DILEMMA	GALL	OPTIMIST
AILING	DIRE	IMPLIED	PERIL
ALIAS	DOCILE	IMPLORED	PRODIGY
APTITUDE	DORY	INAUGURATED	PROXY
ASCERTAIN	EMERGE	INCENTIVE	QUALMS
AWE	ENSCONCED	INDOLENT	REGIMENTATION
BEDLAM	ENSUE	INTERVENE	RIDICULE
CAUCUS	ENTAIL	INVECTIVE	SUBSEQUENT
CONCEDED	EXTRICATE	IRKED	SUBTLE
DEBACLE	FATALISTIC	LURID	SULLEN
DEBUTANTE	FATIGUING	MOCK	SURGEONS
DERELICTS	FEROCITY	MUTUAL	VERGED
DETEST	FORGO	OBTAIN	

Cheaper By The Dozen Vocabulary Word Search 4 Answer Key

AGENDA	DILEMMA	GALL	OPTIMIST
AILING	DIRE	IMPLIED	PERIL
ALIAS	DOCILE	IMPLORED	PRODIGY
APTITUDE	DORY	INAUGURATED	PROXY
ASCERTAIN	EMERGE	INCENTIVE	QUALMS
AWE	ENSCONCED	INDOLENT	REGIMENTATION
BEDLAM	ENSUE	INTERVENE	RIDICULE
CAUCUS	ENTAIL	INVECTIVE	SUBSEQUENT
CONCEDED	EXTRICATE	IRKED	SUBTLE
DEBACLE	FATALISTIC	LURID	SULLEN
DEBUTANTE	FATIGUING	MOCK	SURGEONS
DERELICTS	FEROCITY	MUTUAL	VERGED
DETEST	FORGO	OBTAIN	

Cheaper By The Dozen Vocabulary Crossword 1

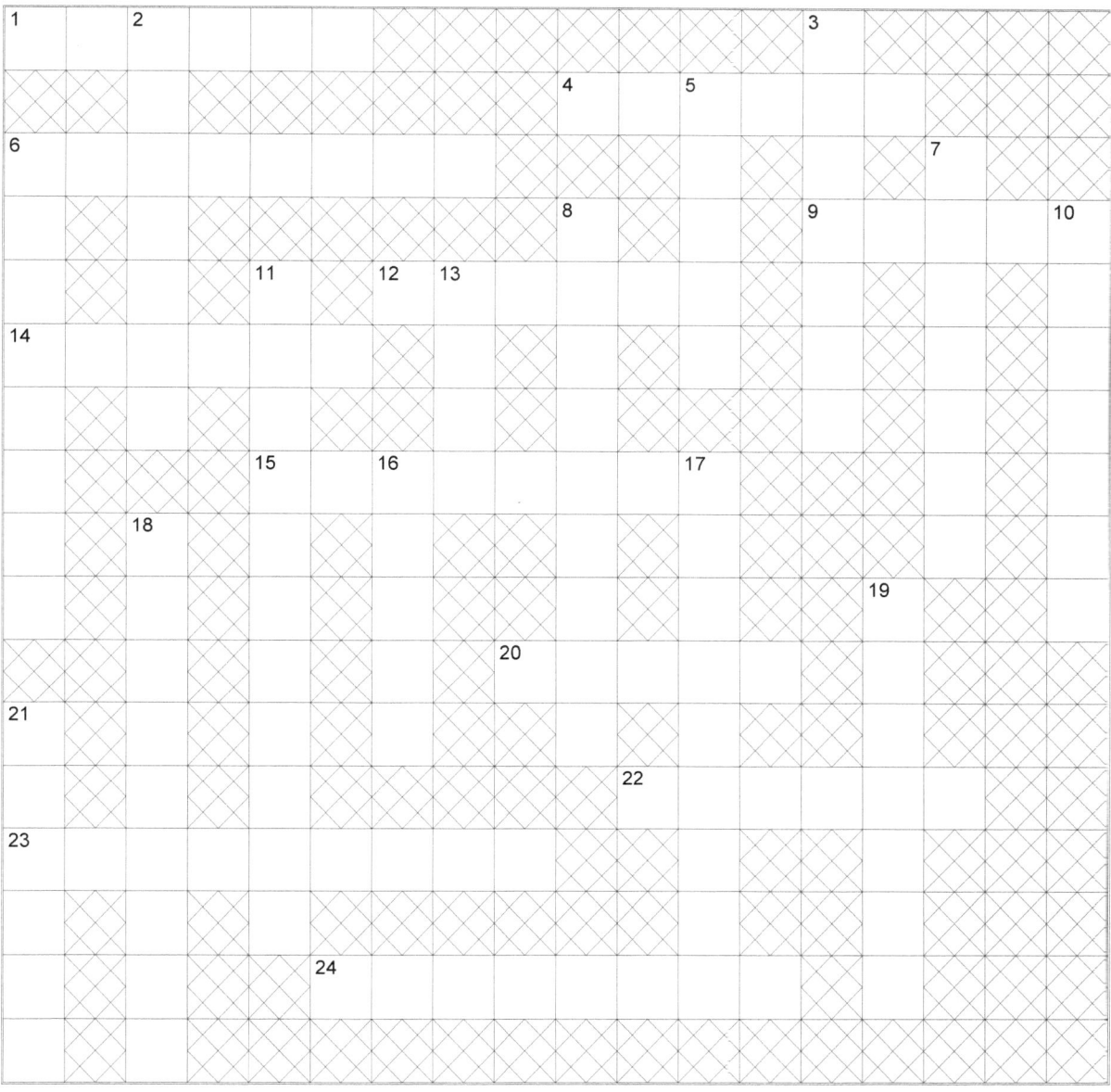

Across
1. Possessed in common
4. Issues causing uneasiness
6. Neighborhood; area
9. Causing shock or horror
12. List of things to be done
14. Ill; sick
15. Begged for urgently
20. To follow immediately after
22. A meeting to decide upon questions of policy
23. Social outcasts
24. Admitted; acknowledged as true

Down
2. Without speaking
3. Suggested without directly saying
5. An assumed name
6. Truthfulness
7. Person with exceptional talents
8. To come between; interfere
10. Disaster
11. Angrily because of something unjust
13. Self-assertiveness
16. Person authorized to act for another
17. Young woman who is formally presented to society
18. Laughable because it's ridiculous or foolish
19. Accompanied by or filled with something undesirable
21. Noisy uproar and confusion

Cheaper By The Dozen Vocabulary Crossword 1 Answer Key

	1 M	U	2 T	U	A	L						3 I		
			A					4 Q	5 U	A	L	M	S	
6 V	I	C	I	N	I	T	Y		L		P		7 P	
E			I					8 I	I		9 L	U	R	10 D
R			T		11 I	12 A	13 G	E	N	D	A		O	E
14 A	I	L	I	N	G		A		T		S		D	B
C			Y		D		L		E			D	I	A
I				15 I	M	16 P	L	O	R	E	17 D		G	C
T		18 L		G		R		V			E		Y	L
Y		U		N		O		E			B		19 F	E
		D		A		X		20 E	N	S	U	E	R	
21 B		I		N		Y		E			T		A	
E		C		T				22 C	A	U	C	U	S	
23 D	E	R	E	L	I	C	T	S			N		G	
L		O		Y							T		H	
A		U		24 C	O	N	C	E	D	E	D		T	
M		S												

Across
1. Possessed in common
4. Issues causing uneasiness
6. Neighborhood; area
9. Causing shock or horror
12. List of things to be done
14. Ill; sick
15. Begged for urgently
20. To follow immediately after
22. A meeting to decide upon questions of policy
23. Social outcasts
24. Admitted; acknowledged as true

Down
2. Without speaking
3. Suggested without directly saying
5. An assumed name
6. Truthfulness
7. Person with exceptional talents
8. To come between; interfere
10. Disaster
11. Angrily because of something unjust
13. Self-assertiveness
16. Person authorized to act for another
17. Young woman who is formally presented to society
18. Laughable because it's ridiculous or foolish
19. Accompanied by or filled with something undesirable
21. Noisy uproar and confusion

Cheaper By The Dozen Vocabulary Crossword 2

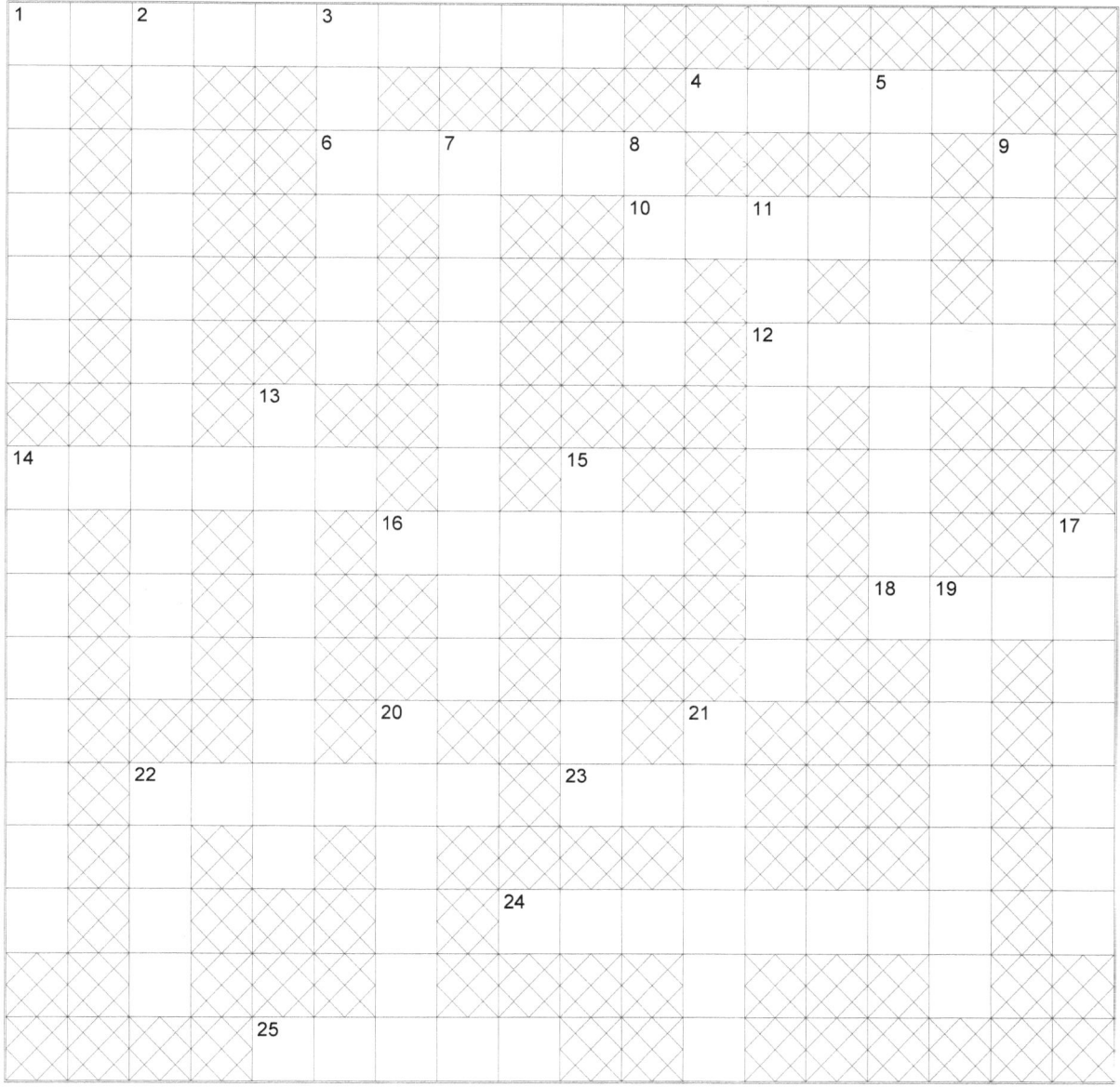

Across
1. Following in order
4. Irritated; annoyed
6. Ill; sick
10. An assumed name
12. Person authorized to act for another
14. Came to the edge of
16. Give up
18. Terrible; disastrous
22. Possessed in common
23. An emotion of respect and wonder tinged with fear
24. Musical keyboard fitted with steam whistles
25. To follow immediately after

Down
1. Showing ill-humor or resentment
2. Aggressive; hostile
3. Issues causing uneasiness
5. Settled securely
7. Laughable because it's ridiculous or foolish
8. Self-assertiveness
9. Small, narrow, flat-bottomed boat
11. Begged for urgently
13. Savage fierceness
14. Truthfulness
15. List of things to be done
17. Disaster
19. Suggested without directly saying
20. A meeting to decide upon questions of policy
21. Noisy uproar and confusion
22. Imitation; false

Cheaper By The Dozen Vocabulary Crossword 2 Answer Key

Across
1. Following in order
4. Irritated; annoyed
6. Ill; sick
10. An assumed name
12. Person authorized to act for another
14. Came to the edge of
16. Give up
18. Terrible; disastrous
22. Possessed in common
23. An emotion of respect and wonder tinged with fear
24. Musical keyboard fitted with steam whistles
25. To follow immediately after

Down
1. Showing ill-humor or resentment
2. Aggressive; hostile
3. Issues causing uneasiness
5. Settled securely
7. Laughable because it's ridiculous or foolish
8. Self-assertiveness
9. Small, narrow, flat-bottomed boat
11. Begged for urgently
13. Savage fierceness
14. Truthfulness
15. List of things to be done
17. Disaster
19. Suggested without directly saying
20. A meeting to decide upon questions of policy
21. Noisy uproar and confusion
22. Imitation; false

Cheaper By The Dozen Vocabulary Crossword 3

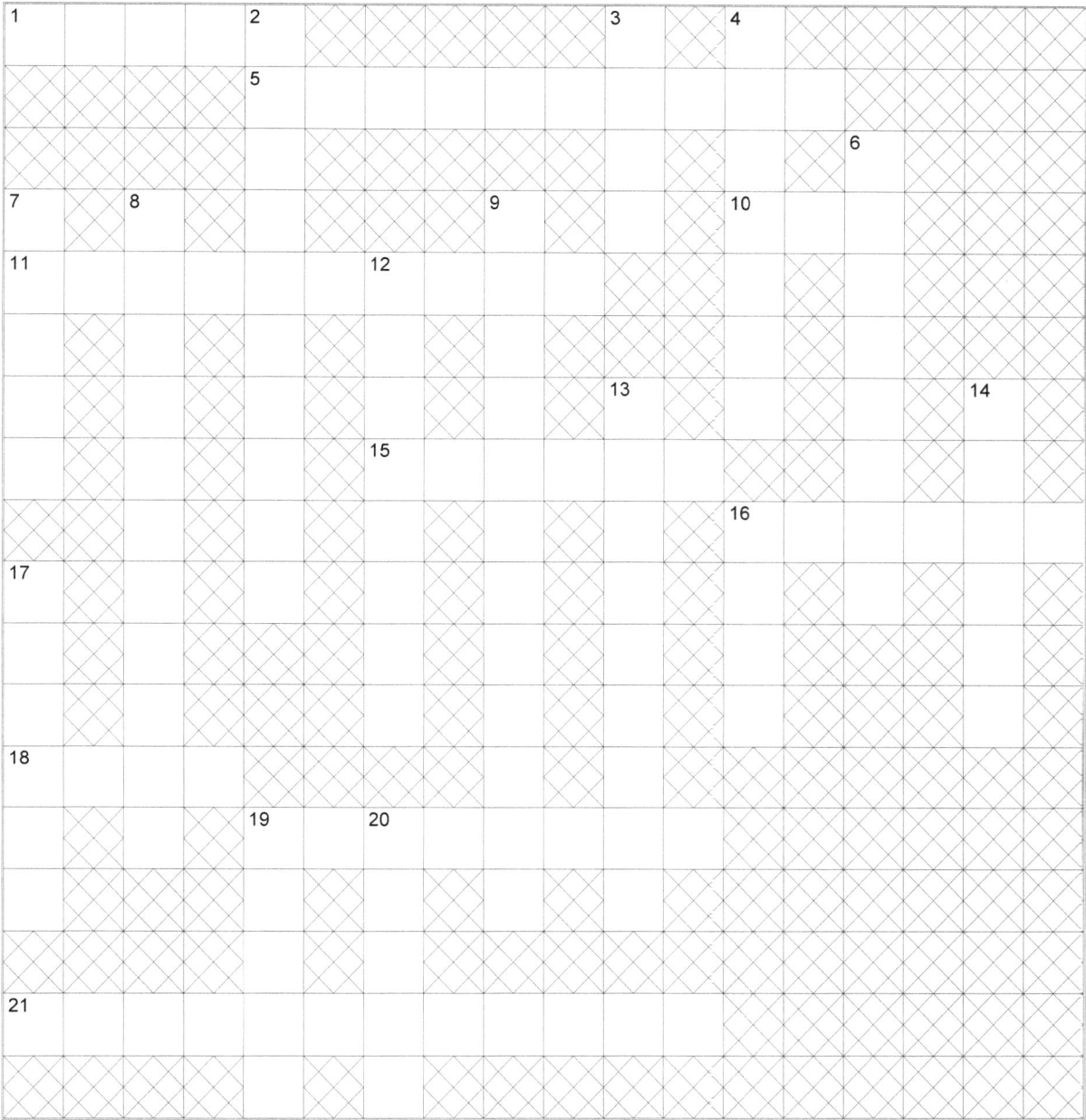

Across
1. An assumed name
5. Not returned
10. An emotion of respect and wonder tinged with fear
11. Prearranged meeting
15. Ill; sick
16. Possessed in common
18. Self-assertiveness
19. Begged for urgently
21. Grateful

Down
2. Following in order
3. Terrible; disastrous
4. Disaster
6. Savage fierceness
7. Person authorized to act for another
8. Angrily because of something unjust
9. Prayer; humble begging
12. Truthfulness
13. Settled securely
14. Issues causing uneasiness
16. Imitation; false
17. Came to the edge of
19. Irritated; annoyed
20. Danger

Cheaper By The Dozen Vocabulary Crossword 3 Answer Key

Across
1. An assumed name
5. Not returned
10. An emotion of respect and wonder tinged with fear
11. Prearranged meeting
15. Ill; sick
16. Possessed in common
18. Self-assertiveness
19. Begged for urgently
21. Grateful

Down
2. Following in order
3. Terrible; disastrous
4. Disaster
6. Savage fierceness
7. Person authorized to act for another
8. Angrily because of something unjust
9. Prayer; humble begging
12. Truthfulness
13. Settled securely
14. Issues causing uneasiness
16. Imitation; false
17. Came to the edge of
19. Irritated; annoyed
20. Danger

Cheaper By The Dozen Vocabulary Crossword 4

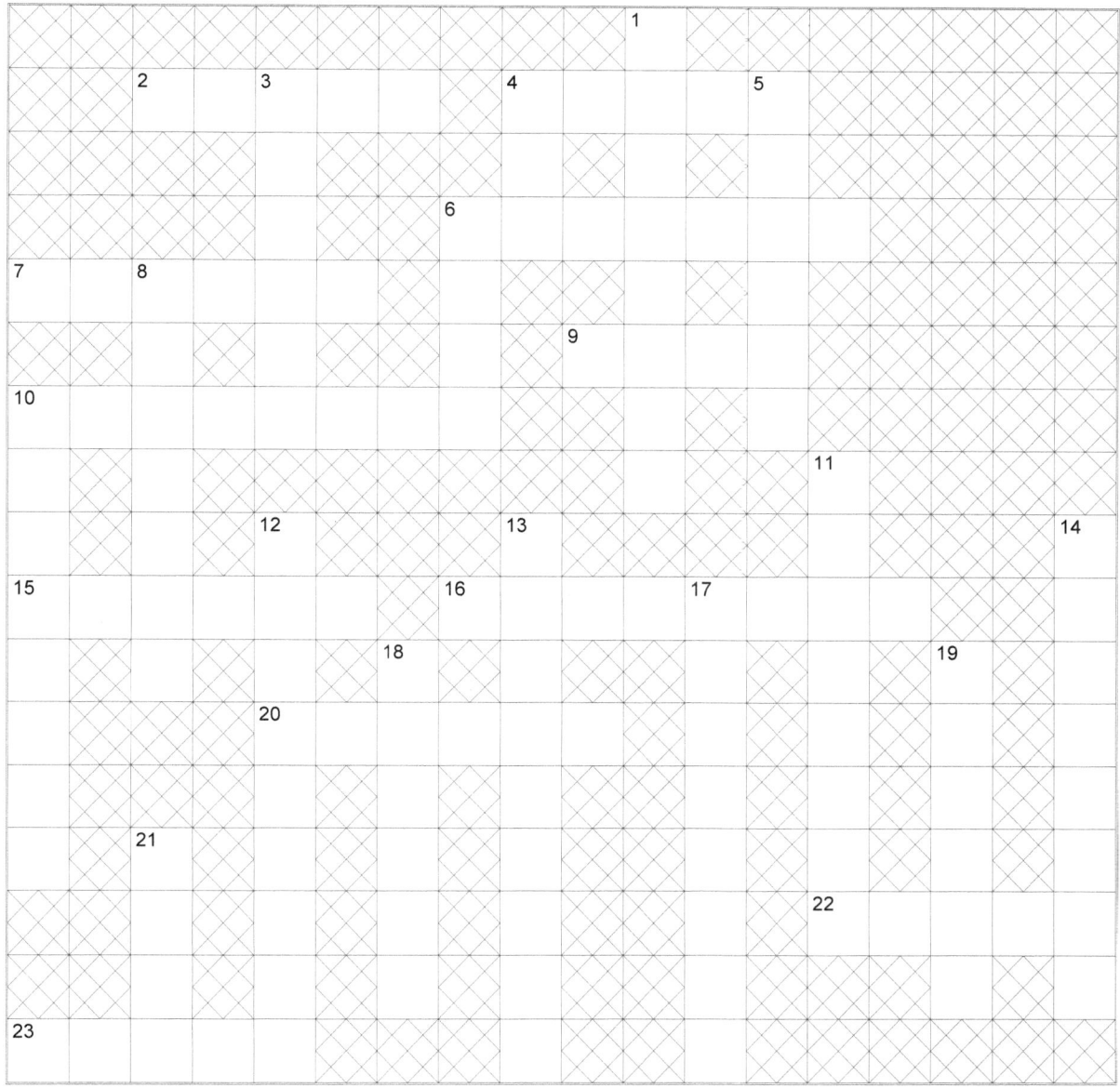

Across
2. Person authorized to act for another
4. An assumed name
6. Disaster
7. Possessed in common
9. Terrible; disastrous
10. Neighborhood; area
15. Ill; sick
16. Savage fierceness
20. A meeting to decide upon questions of policy
22. To follow immediately after
23. Irritated; annoyed

Down
1. Energy
3. Get; acquire
4. An emotion of respect and wonder tinged with fear
5. Showing ill-humor or resentment
6. Small, narrow, flat-bottomed boat
8. Without speaking
10. Truthfulness
11. Ability
12. Settled securely
13. Young woman who is formally presented to society
14. Begged for urgently
17. Admitted; acknowledged as true
18. Issues causing uneasiness
19. Dislike intensely
21. Imitation; false

Cheaper By The Dozen Vocabulary Crossword 4 Answer Key

							V				
	P	R	O	X	Y	A	L	I	A	S	
			B				W		T	U	
			T			D	E	B	A	C	L	E
M	U	T	U	A	L		O		L		L	
		A		I			R		D	I	R	E
V	I	C	I	N	I	T	Y		T		N	
E		I							Y		A	
R		T		E			D				P		I
A	I	L	I	N	G		F	E	R	O	C	I	T	Y	M
C		Y		S		Q	B			O		I		D	P
I				C	A	U	C	U	S		N		T	E	L
T				O		A	T				C		U	T	O
Y		M		N		L	A				E		D	E	R
		O		C		M	N				D	E	N	S	U	E
		C		E		S	T				E		T	D
I	R	K	E	D			E				D			

Across
2. Person authorized to act for another
4. An assumed name
6. Disaster
7. Possessed in common
9. Terrible; disastrous
10. Neighborhood; area
15. Ill; sick
16. Savage fierceness
20. A meeting to decide upon questions of policy
22. To follow immediately after
23. Irritated; annoyed

Down
1. Energy
3. Get; acquire
4. An emotion of respect and wonder tinged with fear
5. Showing ill-humor or resentment
6. Small, narrow, flat-bottomed boat
8. Without speaking
10. Truthfulness
11. Ability
12. Settled securely
13. Young woman who is formally presented to society
14. Begged for urgently
17. Admitted; acknowledged as true
18. Issues causing uneasiness
19. Dislike intensely
21. Imitation; false

Cheaper By The Dozen Vocabulary Juggle Letters 1

1. CEDPRUDEL = 1. _____
   Prevented; made impossible by previous action

2. AEDIMLM = 2. _____
   A situation requiring a choice

3. EEDZRVOSNU = 3. _____
   Prearranged meeting

4. ACIEYVTR = 4. _____
   Truthfulness

5. NDDECOCE = 5. _____
   Admitted; acknowledged as true

6. LTCATYI = 6. _____
   Without speaking

7. RGFUAHT = 7. _____
   Accompanied by or filled with something undesirable

8. MLNUAOIYSNU = 8. _____
   In complete agreement

9. NNDUSINEEO = 9. _____
   Things (usually negative) implied or suggested

10. ITLACPUTAED =10. _____
    Yielded; gave in

11. XAETRCIET =11. _____
    Release from entanglement

12. KOCM =12. _____
    Imitation; false

13. CPTPRAVEEIIA =13. _____
    Grateful

14. VTEEIVNIC =14. _____
    Insults

15. ENSSUORG =15. _____
    Doctors who perform operations

Cheaper By The Dozen Vocabulary Juggle Letters 1 Answer Key

1. CEDPRUDEL = 1. PRECLUDED
   Prevented; made impossible by previous action

2. AEDIMLM = 2. DILEMMA
   A situation requiring a choice

3. EEDZRVOSNU = 3. RENDEZVOUS
   Prearranged meeting

4. ACIEYVTR = 4. VERACITY
   Truthfulness

5. NDDECOCE = 5. CONCEDED
   Admitted; acknowledged as true

6. LTCATYI = 6. TACITLY
   Without speaking

7. RGFUAHT = 7. FRAUGHT
   Accompanied by or filled with something undesirable

8. MLNUAOIYSNU = 8. UNANIMOUSLY
   In complete agreement

9. NNDUSINEEO = 9. INNUENDOES
   Things (usually negative) implied or suggested

10. ITLACPUTAED = 10. CAPITULATED
    Yielded; gave in

11. XAETRCIET = 11. EXTRICATE
    Release from entanglement

12. KOCM = 12. MOCK
    Imitation; false

13. CPTPRAVEEIIA = 13. APPRECIATIVE
    Grateful

14. VTEEIVNIC = 14. INVECTIVE
    Insults

15. ENSSUORG = 15. SURGEONS
    Doctors who perform operations

Cheaper By The Dozen Vocabulary Juggle Letters 2

1. DTUIPTAE = 1. _____
   Ability

2. ICVEYATR = 2. _____
   Truthfulness

3. IIICTVYN = 3. _____
   Neighborhood; area

4. ETNRNPEAT = 4. _____
   Feeling sorry for a wrong-doing

5. LEROATET = 5. _____
   Allow without opposing

6. PRIRIOUTSESUT = 6. _____
   Performed or acquired by secret means

7. YUUMSNANOIL = 7. _____
   In complete agreement

8. ENUES = 8. _____
   To follow immediately after

9. PIERDRMAN = 9. _____
   A scolding, punishment or correction for doing something wrong

10. AAENTSCIR = 10. _____
    Find out

11. ERFONRECD = 11. _____
    Bestowed or given as an honor

12. NNEIVTICE = 12. _____
    A reward offered to motivate one to action

13. USCCUA = 13. _____
    A meeting to decide upon questions of policy

14. EATECRIXT = 14. _____
    Release from entanglement

15. SAILA = 15. _____
    An assumed name

Cheaper By The Dozen Vocabulary Juggle Letters 2 Answer Key

1. DTUIPTAE = 1. APTITUDE
Ability

2. ICVEYATR = 2. VERACITY
Truthfulness

3. IIICTVYN = 3. VICINITY
Neighborhood; area

4. ETNRNPEAT = 4. REPENTANT
Feeling sorry for a wrong-doing

5. LEROATET = 5. TOLERATE
Allow without opposing

6. PRIRIOUTSESUT = 6. SURREPTITIOUS
Performed or acquired by secret means

7. YUUMSNANOIL = 7. UNANIMOUSLY
In complete agreement

8. ENUES = 8. ENSUE
To follow immediately after

9. PIERDRMAN = 9. REPRIMAND
A scolding, punishment or correction for doing something wrong

10. AAENTSCIR = 10. ASCERTAIN
Find out

11. ERFONRECD = 11. CONFERRED
Bestowed or given as an honor

12. NNEIVTICE = 12. INCENTIVE
A reward offered to motivate one to action

13. USCCUA = 13. CAUCUS
A meeting to decide upon questions of policy

14. EATECRIXT = 14. EXTRICATE
Release from entanglement

15. SAILA = 15. ALIAS
An assumed name

Cheaper By The Dozen Vocabulary Juggle Letters 3

1. ORTELAET = 1. _____
   Allow without opposing

2. AALSI = 2. _____
   An assumed name

3. ELRICDIU = 3. _____
   Make fun of

4. LODIPMER = 4. _____
   Begged for urgently

5. AEUDTATIPLC = 5. _____
   Yielded; gave in

6. EIRD = 6. _____
   Terrible; disastrous

7. YCIIITVN = 7. _____
   Neighborhood; area

8. GOEUSRNS = 8. _____
   Doctors who perform operations

9. ABMDEL = 9. _____
   Noisy uproar and confusion

10. OILULNSYCEDUR = 10. _____
    Expressing disbelief

11. IAREPCETPIVA = 11. _____
    Grateful

12. CMKO = 12. _____
    Imitation; false

13. SDTTEE = 13. _____
    Dislike intensely

14. NCTEIEVIV = 14. _____
    Insults

15. SIOTMPIT = 15. _____
    One who always expects a favorable outcome

Cheaper By The Dozen Vocabulary Juggle Letters 3 Answer Key

1. ORTELAET = 1. TOLERATE
Allow without opposing

2. AALSI = 2. ALIAS
An assumed name

3. ELRICDIU = 3. RIDICULE
Make fun of

4. LODIPMER = 4. IMPLORED
Begged for urgently

5. AEUDTATIPLC = 5. CAPITULATED
Yielded; gave in

6. EIRD = 6. DIRE
Terrible; disastrous

7. YCIIITVN = 7. VICINITY
Neighborhood; area

8. GOEUSRNS = 8. SURGEONS
Doctors who perform operations

9. ABMDEL = 9. BEDLAM
Noisy uproar and confusion

10. OILULNSYCEDUR = 10. INCREDULOUSLY
Expressing disbelief

11. IAREPCETPIVA = 11. APPRECIATIVE
Grateful

12. CMKO = 12. MOCK
Imitation; false

13. SDTTEE = 13. DETEST
Dislike intensely

14. NCTEIEVIV = 14. INVECTIVE
Insults

15. SIOTMPIT = 15. OPTIMIST
One who always expects a favorable outcome

Cheaper By The Dozen Vocabulary Juggle Letters 4

1. UISRESITORPTU = 1. _____
   Performed or acquired by secret means

2. TABNIO = 2. _____
   Get; acquire

3. EIVCNEITV = 3. _____
   Insults

4. UELBTS = 4. _____
   Not immediately obvious

5. RILHEORCAT = 5. _____
   Only one or no answer is expected

6. PMANERRDI = 6. _____
   A scolding, punishment or correction for doing something wrong

7. ETSUUNBSQE = 7. _____
   Following in order

8. ETTXEACIR = 8. _____
   Release from entanglement

9. TPERUAELP = 9. _____
   Lasting forever

10. EAW = 10. _____
    An emotion of respect and wonder tinged with fear

11. ICVNTENEI = 11. _____
    A reward offered to motivate one to action

12. YGRDIOP = 12. _____
    Person with exceptional talents

13. DVCGEERNO = 13. _____
    Approached the same point from different directions

14. NDUNSENOIE = 14. _____
    Things (usually negative) implied or suggested

15. YDOR = 15. _____
    Small, narrow, flat-bottomed boat

Cheaper By The Dozen Vocabulary Juggle Leters 4 Answer Key

1. UISRESITORPTU = 1. SURREPTITIOUS
   Performed or acquired by secret means

2. TABNIO = 2. OBTAIN
   Get; acquire

3. EIVCNEITV = 3. INVECTIVE
   Insults

4. UELBTS = 4. SUBTLE
   Not immediately obvious

5. RILHEORCAT = 5. RHETORICAL
   Only one or no answer is expected

6. PMANERRDI = 6. REPRIMAND
   A scolding, punishment or correction for doing something wrong

7. ETSUUNBSQE = 7. SUBSEQUENT
   Following in order

8. ETTXEACIR = 8. EXTRICATE
   Release from entanglement

9. TPERUAELP = 9. PERPETUAL
   Lasting forever

10. EAW = 10. AWE
    An emotion of respect and wonder tinged with fear

11. ICVNTENEI = 11. INCENTIVE
    A reward offered to motivate one to action

12. YGRDIOP = 12. PRODIGY
    Person with exceptional talents

13. DVCGEERNO = 13. CONVERGED
    Approached the same point from different directions

14. NDUNSENOIE = 14. INNUENDOES
    Things (usually negative) implied or suggested

15. YDOR = 15. DORY
    Small, narrow, flat-bottomed boat

ADMONISHED	Kindly but seriously reprimanded
AGENDA	List of things to be done
AILING	Ill; sick
ALIAS	An assumed name
APPRECIATIVE	Grateful
APTITUDE	Ability

ASCERTAIN	Find out
ATROCIOUS	Exceptionally bad
AWE	An emotion of respect and wonder tinged with fear
BEDLAM	Noisy uproar and confusion
BELLIGERENT	Aggressive; hostile
BENEVOLENT	Kind; charitable

CALLIOPE	Musical keyboard fitted with steam whistles
CAPITULATED	Yielded; gave in
CAUCUS	A meeting to decide upon questions of policy
COINCIDE	To happen at the same time
CONCEDED	Admitted; acknowledged as true
CONFERRED	Bestowed or given as an honor

CONTAGIOUS	Tending to spread from one to another
CONVENT	Home for nuns
CONVERGED	Approached the same point from different directions
CONVICTION	Strong belief
DEBACLE	Disaster
DEBUTANTE	Young woman who is formally presented to society

DELECTABLE	Enjoyable; delightful
DERELICTS	Social outcasts
DETEST	Dislike intensely
DILEMMA	A situation requiring a choice
DIRE	Terrible; disastrous
DOCILE	Obedient; submissive to management

DORY	Small, narrow, flat-bottomed boat
EMERGE	To come forth from; come into sight
ENSCONCED	Settled securely
ENSUE	To follow immediately after
ENTAIL	To have a necessary accompaniment or consequences
EXTRICATE	Release from entanglement

FATALISTIC	Belief that events are predetermined; submission to fate
FATIGUING	Tiring
FEROCITY	Savage fierceness
FORGO	Give up
FRAUGHT	Accompanied by or filled with something undesirable
GALL	Self-assertiveness

IMPLIED	Suggested without directly saying
IMPLORED	Begged for urgently
INAUGURATED	Began
INCENTIVE	A reward offered to motivate one to action
INCREDULOUSLY	Expressing disbelief
INDICATE	Demonstrate or point out

INDIGNANTLY	Angrily because of something unjust
INDOLENT	Lazy
INEVITABLE	Unavoidable; going to happen no matter what
INNOCUOUS	Harmless
INNUENDOES	Things (usually negative) implied or suggested
INTERVENE	To come between; interfere

INTRICACIES	Many complexly arranged elements
INVECTIVE	Insults
IRKED	Irritated; annoyed
LUDICROUS	Laughable because it's ridiculous or foolish
LURID	Causing shock or horror
MOCK	Imitation; false

MUTINOUS	Rebellious
MUTUAL	Possessed in common
OBTAIN	Get; acquire
OMINOUSLY	Threateningly
OPTIMIST	One who always expects a favorable outcome
PERIL	Danger

PERPETUAL	Lasting forever
PHILANTHROPY	Giving charitable donations or aid
PRECISELY	Exactly
PRECLUDED	Prevented; made impossible by previous action
PRELUDE	Event or action preceding a more important one
PRODIGY	Person with exceptional talents

PROXY	Person authorized to act for another
QUALMS	Issues causing uneasiness
REGIMENTATION	Uniformity and discipline
RENDEZVOUS	Prearranged meeting
REPENTANT	Feeling sorry for a wrong-doing
REPRIMAND	A scolding, punishment or correction for doing something wrong

REPROBATES	Morally unprincipled people
RHETORICAL	Only one or no answer is expected
RIDICULE	Make fun of
SIMULTANEOUS	At the same time
SUBSEQUENT	Following in order
SUBTLE	Not immediately obvious

SULLEN	Showing ill-humor or resentment
SUPPLICATION	Prayer; humble begging
SURGEONS	Doctors who perform operations
SURREPTITIOUS	Performed or acquired by secret means
TACITLY	Without speaking
TOLERATE	Allow without opposing

ULTIMATE	Final; best or most extreme example of its kind
UNANIMOUSLY	In complete agreement
UNREQUITED	Not returned
VERACITY	Truthfulness
VERGED	Came to the edge of
VICINITY	Neighborhood; area

VITALITY

Energy

Cheaper By The Dozen Vocabulary

REPRIMAND	APTITUDE	EXTRICATE	VICINITY	ASCERTAIN
IMPLORED	TACITLY	ENTAIL	PRECISELY	DORY
INDOLENT	VERGED	FREE SPACE	INCREDULOUSLY	COINCIDE
DIRE	UNANIMOUSLY	ULTIMATE	REPROBATES	CAPITULATED
SURGEONS	CONFERRED	EMERGE	LURID	PRECLUDED

Cheaper By The Dozen Vocabulary

PRODIGY	DOCILE	CONVICTION	INTRICACIES	ADMONISHED
DETEST	REPENTANT	MOCK	PHILANTHROPY	TOLERATE
PROXY	RENDEZVOUS	FREE SPACE	BENEVOLENT	INEVITABLE
DERELICTS	CONVERGED	UNREQUITED	FATIGUING	FRAUGHT
DELECTABLE	IMPLIED	PRELUDE	ENSUE	IRKED

Cheaper By The Dozen Vocabulary

FORGO	BELLIGERENT	FATIGUING	PRODIGY	DORY
FATALISTIC	OMINOUSLY	DETEST	PERIL	DILEMMA
VITALITY	TOLERATE	FREE SPACE	UNANIMOUSLY	VICINITY
INCREDULOUSLY	DEBACLE	VERGED	SIMULTANEOUS	INAUGURATED
MOCK	REPROBATES	BENEVOLENT	SUBTLE	FRAUGHT

Cheaper By The Dozen Vocabulary

SULLEN	FEROCITY	MUTINOUS	APPRECIATIVE	REPENTANT
DEBUTANTE	COINCIDE	SURGEONS	ULTIMATE	AWE
DELECTABLE	CONVENT	FREE SPACE	INEVITABLE	LURID
SUBSEQUENT	GALL	INCENTIVE	IMPLIED	EXTRICATE
INDICATE	INNOCUOUS	CONVICTION	ADMONISHED	ASCERTAIN

Cheaper By The Dozen Vocabulary

IMPLORED	INEVITABLE	INTRICACIES	MOCK	ULTIMATE
PHILANTHROPY	SUBSEQUENT	INCENTIVE	LUDICROUS	REPRIMAND
RIDICULE	OMINOUSLY	FREE SPACE	EXTRICATE	BEDLAM
CONCEDED	DILEMMA	VICINITY	TACITLY	INCREDULOUSLY
FRAUGHT	VERGED	APPRECIATIVE	IMPLIED	REGIMENTATION

Cheaper By The Dozen Vocabulary

SUPPLICATION	AWE	INVECTIVE	DEBUTANTE	CONVERGED
DOCILE	FEROCITY	CONTAGIOUS	INNOCUOUS	ENTAIL
DERELICTS	REPENTANT	FREE SPACE	REPROBATES	INAUGURATED
FATIGUING	EMERGE	COINCIDE	DETEST	INDICATE
CONVENT	DELECTABLE	ATROCIOUS	AILING	FORGO

Cheaper By The Dozen Vocabulary

INCENTIVE	SUBSEQUENT	FATIGUING	BEDLAM	ENSCONCED
CONVERGED	FRAUGHT	INDICATE	PRODIGY	SURREPTITIOUS
CONCEDED	PERPETUAL	FREE SPACE	TOLERATE	INDIGNANTLY
BELLIGERENT	CONVENT	ALIAS	MOCK	PERIL
VERGED	DILEMMA	IMPLORED	COINCIDE	PRECISELY

Cheaper By The Dozen Vocabulary

DETEST	OPTIMIST	BENEVOLENT	TACITLY	INNOCUOUS
LUDICROUS	REPENTANT	MUTUAL	CALLIOPE	SUPPLICATION
UNREQUITED	INCREDULOUSLY	FREE SPACE	CAPITULATED	OMINOUSLY
DOCILE	RHETORICAL	SUBTLE	INTERVENE	APPRECIATIVE
PRECLUDED	LURID	APTITUDE	VITALITY	RIDICULE

Cheaper By The Dozen Vocabulary

PRECISELY	UNANIMOUSLY	INNUENDOES	MUTINOUS	PHILANTHROPY
EXTRICATE	FORGO	INDOLENT	RENDEZVOUS	QUALMS
SUBSEQUENT	INNOCUOUS	FREE SPACE	ADMONISHED	DELECTABLE
FATALISTIC	ENTAIL	UNREQUITED	DILEMMA	INVECTIVE
GALL	FRAUGHT	LUDICROUS	DEBACLE	DIRE

Cheaper By The Dozen Vocabulary

VERGED	CONFERRED	ASCERTAIN	CAUCUS	OPTIMIST
TACITLY	OMINOUSLY	APPRECIATIVE	CONVERGED	INCENTIVE
AGENDA	DEBUTANTE	FREE SPACE	CALLIOPE	PERPETUAL
EMERGE	APTITUDE	INTRICACIES	INTERVENE	LURID
SUPPLICATION	SULLEN	ALIAS	SURREPTITIOUS	INDIGNANTLY

Cheaper By The Dozen Vocabulary

INTERVENE	EXTRICATE	SUPPLICATION	DOCILE	CONVERGED
AILING	UNREQUITED	REPENTANT	INDIGNANTLY	INCREDULOUSLY
CONVENT	CALLIOPE	FREE SPACE	OPTIMIST	ENTAIL
TOLERATE	ADMONISHED	PRECISELY	DERELICTS	INVECTIVE
DETEST	LUDICROUS	PERIL	IRKED	INAUGURATED

Cheaper By The Dozen Vocabulary

ASCERTAIN	VERGED	GALL	REGIMENTATION	DIRE
CONFERRED	ATROCIOUS	CAPITULATED	MUTINOUS	PHILANTHROPY
INCENTIVE	INDICATE	FREE SPACE	INTRICACIES	RENDEZVOUS
ULTIMATE	MUTUAL	APTITUDE	VITALITY	IMPLIED
CONVICTION	SUBTLE	SUBSEQUENT	DILEMMA	SURGEONS

Cheaper By The Dozen Vocabulary

INDIGNANTLY	LUDICROUS	UNREQUITED	AILING	PRECISELY
ALIAS	OBTAIN	INDICATE	DOCILE	MUTUAL
INDOLENT	DERELICTS	FREE SPACE	ENSCONCED	APTITUDE
RHETORICAL	INNUENDOES	FATIGUING	FEROCITY	DELECTABLE
APPRECIATIVE	CONVENT	CONFERRED	MUTINOUS	CAPITULATED

Cheaper By The Dozen Vocabulary

CONVICTION	CAUCUS	INTRICACIES	AGENDA	CONCEDED
SUBTLE	DIRE	INEVITABLE	DETEST	ENTAIL
INNOCUOUS	PRECLUDED	FREE SPACE	EXTRICATE	OPTIMIST
CONTAGIOUS	BENEVOLENT	PRELUDE	DEBUTANTE	OMINOUSLY
COINCIDE	CALLIOPE	BEDLAM	PRODIGY	REPENTANT

Cheaper By The Dozen Vocabulary

FORGO	INCENTIVE	PRECISELY	INDOLENT	LUDICROUS
ENSCONCED	RIDICULE	SURREPTITIOUS	REGIMENTATION	IRKED
MUTUAL	TACITLY	FREE SPACE	FATIGUING	INCREDULOUSLY
FEROCITY	PERPETUAL	AWE	IMPLORED	ASCERTAIN
SIMULTANEOUS	RHETORICAL	VERGED	DIRE	PRELUDE

Cheaper By The Dozen Vocabulary

FATALISTIC	APTITUDE	CAPITULATED	QUALMS	EXTRICATE
VICINITY	OPTIMIST	INNUENDOES	REPENTANT	INVECTIVE
PROXY	INDIGNANTLY	FREE SPACE	DELECTABLE	CONVERGED
DEBUTANTE	IMPLIED	SULLEN	DETEST	DORY
CONCEDED	INNOCUOUS	AGENDA	GALL	FRAUGHT

Cheaper By The Dozen Vocabulary

PRECLUDED	GALL	BELLIGERENT	RENDEZVOUS	MUTINOUS
AWE	SUBSEQUENT	INTERVENE	OMINOUSLY	IRKED
CONFERRED	DETEST	FREE SPACE	CONVERGED	APTITUDE
ADMONISHED	SURREPTITIOUS	SULLEN	TOLERATE	CAPITULATED
EMERGE	INNOCUOUS	APPRECIATIVE	PRECISELY	DEBACLE

Cheaper By The Dozen Vocabulary

UNANIMOUSLY	INCENTIVE	INTRICACIES	REPENTANT	BEDLAM
ENTAIL	COINCIDE	CONVICTION	ASCERTAIN	INEVITABLE
CALLIOPE	MOCK	FREE SPACE	ULTIMATE	ALIAS
SIMULTANEOUS	DOCILE	DELECTABLE	SUBTLE	OPTIMIST
OBTAIN	RHETORICAL	DIRE	EXTRICATE	CAUCUS

Cheaper By The Dozen Vocabulary

ENSUE	FATIGUING	PHILANTHROPY	CAPITULATED	SUBTLE
INCREDULOUSLY	INVECTIVE	VITALITY	DIRE	ASCERTAIN
INNUENDOES	CONCEDED	FREE SPACE	QUALMS	FRAUGHT
APTITUDE	EMERGE	UNANIMOUSLY	GALL	CAUCUS
LUDICROUS	COINCIDE	AILING	SUBSEQUENT	CONTAGIOUS

Cheaper By The Dozen Vocabulary

TACITLY	MOCK	CALLIOPE	REPROBATES	PRECLUDED
ATROCIOUS	INDICATE	DILEMMA	ADMONISHED	BEDLAM
CONFERRED	FEROCITY	FREE SPACE	INDIGNANTLY	PRELUDE
MUTINOUS	REPRIMAND	FORGO	INEVITABLE	AWE
INCENTIVE	DORY	UNREQUITED	EXTRICATE	CONVENT

Cheaper By The Dozen Vocabulary

INNUENDOES	VERACITY	ADMONISHED	CAPITULATED	MUTUAL
DEBUTANTE	FEROCITY	APTITUDE	INDIGNANTLY	ASCERTAIN
INTRICACIES	EMERGE	FREE SPACE	DEBACLE	REGIMENTATION
GALL	INNOCUOUS	SUPPLICATION	PROXY	PHILANTHROPY
MUTINOUS	IMPLIED	DIRE	RHETORICAL	BEDLAM

Cheaper By The Dozen Vocabulary

BELLIGERENT	INVECTIVE	OPTIMIST	INAUGURATED	CONVENT
FATALISTIC	SIMULTANEOUS	TACITLY	INCENTIVE	CONVERGED
DELECTABLE	PRECLUDED	FREE SPACE	OBTAIN	OMINOUSLY
QUALMS	DILEMMA	AWE	TOLERATE	CAUCUS
FRAUGHT	INCREDULOUSLY	UNREQUITED	REPROBATES	PRODIGY

Cheaper By The Dozen Vocabulary

FRAUGHT	CONCEDED	FORGO	SULLEN	GALL
SURREPTITIOUS	INEVITABLE	MOCK	BEDLAM	ULTIMATE
ADMONISHED	QUALMS	FREE SPACE	SURGEONS	PERIL
PHILANTHROPY	ENSCONCED	SUBTLE	INNOCUOUS	LUDICROUS
REPROBATES	INDIGNANTLY	TACITLY	MUTINOUS	VERACITY

Cheaper By The Dozen Vocabulary

UNANIMOUSLY	UNREQUITED	DEBACLE	RHETORICAL	FATALISTIC
OPTIMIST	INVECTIVE	PRECLUDED	DORY	VICINITY
REPENTANT	INDOLENT	FREE SPACE	FEROCITY	AWE
DILEMMA	INCENTIVE	INNUENDOES	APTITUDE	TOLERATE
PERPETUAL	OBTAIN	ENSUE	CAPITULATED	CONTAGIOUS

Cheaper By The Dozen Vocabulary

IMPLORED	DELECTABLE	BENEVOLENT	INDICATE	DETEST
FATIGUING	CONVERGED	PERPETUAL	REGIMENTATION	ASCERTAIN
DERELICTS	UNANIMOUSLY	FREE SPACE	AWE	PHILANTHROPY
DIRE	TOLERATE	SURGEONS	PRODIGY	INNUENDOES
ENSUE	CONFERRED	REPENTANT	EMERGE	CAUCUS

Cheaper By The Dozen Vocabulary

OMINOUSLY	BEDLAM	CONCEDED	PROXY	INAUGURATED
OBTAIN	CONVENT	INNOCUOUS	MUTUAL	SUBSEQUENT
INTRICACIES	CAPITULATED	FREE SPACE	REPROBATES	APPRECIATIVE
FORGO	MUTINOUS	SUPPLICATION	AGENDA	QUALMS
LURID	BELLIGERENT	CONVICTION	VERGED	RIDICULE

Cheaper By The Dozen Vocabulary

REPRIMAND	PHILANTHROPY	IRKED	INAUGURATED	REGIMENTATION
RIDICULE	FORGO	INEVITABLE	EXTRICATE	BELLIGERENT
CAPITULATED	OBTAIN	FREE SPACE	CONVICTION	PRECISELY
CONFERRED	INCENTIVE	APPRECIATIVE	ENSCONCED	INNUENDOES
DILEMMA	AILING	VITALITY	SUPPLICATION	AWE

Cheaper By The Dozen Vocabulary

MOCK	CONTAGIOUS	AGENDA	SURREPTITIOUS	DEBUTANTE
RHETORICAL	CALLIOPE	FATIGUING	PRECLUDED	TOLERATE
GALL	ATROCIOUS	FREE SPACE	BENEVOLENT	OMINOUSLY
EMERGE	VICINITY	DEBACLE	REPROBATES	SULLEN
ASCERTAIN	MUTINOUS	ULTIMATE	SUBTLE	INCREDULOUSLY

Cheaper By The Dozen Vocabulary

BELLIGERENT	RIDICULE	INDOLENT	MUTUAL	DEBACLE
CONTAGIOUS	ATROCIOUS	ALIAS	SIMULTANEOUS	REPENTANT
VERGED	TOLERATE	FREE SPACE	AGENDA	CONVENT
UNREQUITED	CAUCUS	DERELICTS	PROXY	MUTINOUS
INNOCUOUS	DEBUTANTE	OPTIMIST	MOCK	OMINOUSLY

Cheaper By The Dozen Vocabulary

VICINITY	INAUGURATED	FEROCITY	PERPETUAL	DELECTABLE
CONVERGED	FORGO	INCREDULOUSLY	INVECTIVE	VERACITY
CAPITULATED	FATIGUING	FREE SPACE	REPROBATES	REGIMENTATION
IMPLIED	GALL	ADMONISHED	PRELUDE	APPRECIATIVE
FRAUGHT	DOCILE	CONFERRED	UNANIMOUSLY	QUALMS

Cheaper By The Dozen Vocabulary

CONVICTION	LURID	RENDEZVOUS	REPENTANT	FEROCITY
BELLIGERENT	UNANIMOUSLY	CALLIOPE	FATALISTIC	SIMULTANEOUS
DIRE	IRKED	FREE SPACE	PERPETUAL	IMPLIED
DERELICTS	ENSCONCED	EXTRICATE	COINCIDE	CONVENT
SURREPTITIOUS	AILING	DILEMMA	ENTAIL	CONVERGED

Cheaper By The Dozen Vocabulary

DETEST	FRAUGHT	SULLEN	DORY	ATROCIOUS
INNOCUOUS	VERGED	PRECLUDED	ENSUE	GALL
INCREDULOUSLY	VITALITY	FREE SPACE	VICINITY	UNREQUITED
MOCK	INCENTIVE	EMERGE	APTITUDE	DEBUTANTE
TACITLY	PERIL	ULTIMATE	AWE	INVECTIVE